TAROT

Explains the Journey of every Soul...

notionpress
.com

TAROT

Explains the Journey of every Soul...

Priti Wonder

notionpress
.com

Notion Press

5 Muthu Kalathy Street, Triplicane,

Chennai - 600 005

First Published by Notion Press 2014

ISBN: 978-93-84391-81-2

- By Priti Wonder

Tarot Reader, Angel Reader,

Past Life Regression Therapist

Self-trained Life Coach (and Loving it!)

Dedicated to my Dolly Mumma and Sweetheart Daddy Bear..... I'm so thankful I have been gifted by God with such lovely cutie-pies. Every child on earth needs these special pair of people to make their life Magical..

Also to my sweetheart sister, *for* making me *feel*, Im the best person in this World!

Contents

Ackowledgments

I would like to thank my parents first of all, to give me that special time so that I could write this book. They helped me be comfy as much as possible. There were several occasions where me being there in the family picture was necessary but, my mom and dad just let me be and gave me ample time to what I was planning to do. Its a huge thing that only parents can do, to trust upon their kids and be there with them when they actually don't have an idea, what their children are actually planning or aiming in their life. Which is the sole reason why I feel God made parents, because all of us need such support and trust in our lives time and again.

Also thanks to those close family members & friends who had no idea why I was staying away from people, when I was writing this book. It is quite difficult to tackle loads of people when you are doing something like this for the first time. Also I had no idea whether I would be publishing this book or not.

A Special thanks to Mehul Patel for helping me with editing & proofreading for this book. This really took away a lot of burden from my mind. Also to my friends whom I asked at the final hours before publishing, to give a quick check through the book.

All my lovely sweethearts who are like a family to me Aunty Dami, Dardhudidi, Darshuben, you all are just awesome. Darshudidi & Darshuben for being my friends rather then cousins. Aunty Dami for seeing that superstar in me all the time. And all the people who have been quite supportive, and caring. Its not possible to write all the names over here. But I did think about you when I wrote this. Also a huge thanks to my Nautanki Friends, your love and crazy support counts a lot!

I would like to thank to all my teachers who have taught me Tarot directly as well as indirectly what struck me naturally. I have learnt to be confident, and presentable as a professional; because of you. Also to Life who is the biggest teacher, life's lessons are not tough. They are fun, fun when you try to search a lesson in it; and not when you see it as a burden.

And I also believe that clients who have come to me for readings have taught me reading the Tarot equally better as to what I could learn it from teachers. Believe it or not their problems actually helped me to polish my skills and expertise with Tarot.

I thank people who believed in me though not knowing me neither knowing about my tarot skills, it takes huge amount of courage to place your trust in somebody whom you don't know. I did try my best to give you the best and satisfactory answers. And you are responsible for my Tarot journey as your trust helped me to carry on this journey with Tarot reading profession on and on. There were times when I too did have to re-question my profession but a timely client again proved that even nature supports me being in this profession. Thanks to wonderful people, wonderful cards that helped me and wonderful nature, that made it all possible for me and you to better our lives by connecting with each other.

Thanks for the support from my Tarot reader friends from Mumbai and Gujarat that helped me in this profession.

And above all a lovely thanks to the lovely spiritual guidance that guided me into this profession, which has been deeply fulfilling for me.

Author's Note

I began writing my blog for learning Tarot for free in October 2012 which I never thought in the wildest of my dreams to take shape as a book. It still feels so magical how this whole project is happening to me, all so in a miraculous way, as well as unexpectedly. There are for sure blessings of thousands working on this project, and maybe, inner quest and prayers of thousands to get this knowledge to them, which is contained in this book.

I began my tarot journey since 2005 and never took it seriously till 2008. It was just a hobby I used for helping family and friends. Until Tarot Reading Profession 'actually became my profession'. Yeah I do accept it I got clients before I could decide that I am a 'Professional Tarot Reader'. Sounds funny right! But actually at the time there were a few people who didn't know me much but were in a lot of trouble. So they became my regular clients after which their friends too wanted me to read for them. So this is how my Tarot Reading journey began, a little unsure yet satisfying as I could see my client's lives improving. It was the best compliment a Tarot Reader can have.

This book is very special to me as I have put in a lot of hard-work and sittings which usually were not possible for a person like me to do it, that too especially at the time when I started writing about it.

The book is actually helpful for tarot as well as non-tarot enthusiasts as I have included 'Journey of a Soul' which every human needs to know, also termed as "Fool's Journey". How everybody begins as a 'fool' and when they master their lives they stand successful in every area of life.

Along with publishing this book I also am aspiring to write something more in future that will help people better their lives.

So just keep a watch for it.

Until then, this book is dedicated to you. Read it, re-read it.... digest it to the full. Even if you don't want to learn Tarot it is going to help you better your journey in life.

For the Tarot lovers this book will help you get a spiritual connection to your cards helping you to better your skills and giving satisfactory results to your client's.

Thanks & Love you for buying my book, and considering me worthy of adding wonderful nuggets of knowledge to your mind and to your life.

- Priti Wonder

Tarot Reading Essentials

Tarot Reading is a tool for divination, for getting deeper knowledge about any issue and to get advice about any pressing issue of your life.

These cards work with your energy level and your subconscious mind and so there are certain rules for storing your deck.

To learn Tarot Reading all you need to have is a nice beginner's Tarot Deck and a useful and informative book like the one you are holding in your hands. Apart from this book I would recommend that you read more books, as it will help to build your conversation base with your client.

Beginner's Decks

A Beginner's deck is a deck with Basic design and core Rider-Waite theme following. These decks appear crude and simple yet they are very helpful to every beginner due to their simplistic design and simple easy-to-grasp approach.

These decks can be bought as per your choice.

I would recommend you to *buy a deck which attracts you*. Though advanced decks are more attractive they tend to confuse beginners as they have a lot more symbolism added to them according to the theme they are based on along with the Rider-Waite theme. After reading this, if you still feel an advanced deck is for you, then go for it.

Some good beginner's decks are

Rider Waite Tarot Deck, by A.E.Waite

Radiant Rider Waite Tarot Deck, by

Universal Waite Tarot, by

Universal Tarot Professional, by

Advanced Deck's

Advanced decks are the one's which are based on Rider-Waite theme and have an added theme. Like the Shadows capes Tarot, Legacy of the Divine Tarot, Sacred India Tarot by Rohit Arya, Gilded Tarot etc. These decks are very attractive. Their sole purpose is to help the reader attach their intuition with the cards as some people cannot accept simple decks. Though for this reason itself the other Rider Waite deck clones were published. Some good advanced decks are listed in Tarot Resources section at the end of this book.

Storing and Caring about your Deck

Storing and caring about your deck is very important, as this deck is going to be priceless once you start working with it and because it will be absorbing your personal energies to make it unique to you. While Tarot Reader's prefer using a single deck for many many years to come, some also believe to use a deck for entire lifetime. This is not possible as it's difficult to store the deck and use it carefully up till this time.

Tarot Deck carries your vibes and this is how you can connect your intuition with it. So you also need to store the deck well so that your energies are preserved well in the deck, which is going to help you give better readings when your energies are retained within the deck for longer time. Ironically, if the deck gets tattered they know how much 'invaluable' it has become.

I usually laminate my cards to make them durable.

Some normal storing /caring instructions that are usually given by all Tarot Readers

- Store your deck in a wooden box, which usually is very well made without any metal fittings. This will help to preserve the energy of the deck intact after you have finished working with your deck (This kind of wooden box is usually difficult to find, in this case plastic box also serves this purpose.) Also you can use satin pouches to store. I use pouches as well as plastic boxes to store mine.
- Wrap your deck with purple or black coloured cloth, which is usually silk or velvet. This material is said to have power to dispel other external energies from penetrating the deck. And the colours are also believed to be helping with keep negative energies away, and maintaining a positive energy for deck (usually believed for purple colour.) I usually advice my tarot students to choose their favorite color.

- Don't allow anybody to touch the deck without your permission. Also, allow your clients to touch the deck only after you permit them.

  [This is because people have energies that might be low and which might affect the energy of the deck. So when you ultimately allow them, they will be limiting transferring them as now they would be touching the deck only with intention of getting positive answer about their negative situation.]

- The above two should be strictly followed and you can add some crystals or shells or dried herbs with your deck which is said to maintain a high energy level of the cards.

- Furthermore, don't store your deck near electricity lines as they too interfere with the charge of the deck.

These are the general rules, follow them which resonates with you. If you feel like adding some more to them don't hesitate. Tarot will get more personalized when you add your personal touch to these rules. Also these rules are meant to make cards more relative to you. Don't follow them out of fear. Tarot is spiritual and not scary. Divine energy talks through Tarot and so be as comfortable as you can be with your cards. Divine loves you and wants you to go easy on life through the cards.

Charging the Deck to make it Personal

The deck which is factory packed doesn't have your vibes, you need to charge it in order to make it personal so that it is uniquely *your* deck, and gives you answers from your intuition. For this you need to carry it with you all the time for at least 21 days. I still do it even after years of buying the deck. Carry it wherever you go to the market, to work and even to the loo.

Also do this regularly as your deck would absorb other people's energies, usually negative that would drain the deck's energy low in long run; if it's not worked upon.

Imagine a shaft of bright white light coming down from heaven into your deck, and all low and negative energy is getting out from your deck in the form of smoke, dirt or dirty coloured liquid. Once the deck is clean the dirty colours and icky feeling will disappear and deck will appear glowing with the divine energy from heaven. The deck is now cleansed and energized. Well if you are totally new to what you are reading just imagine this happening and it would happen.

[If you become a professional tarot reader fetching more then 15-20 readings per day from your deck, it will make your deck over-weighty with negative and blocked energies probably from your clients who feel this way; so you need to do this cleansing daily to help your deck stay 'healthy'. As a healthy deck will help you give better and healthier readings.

By healthy readings I mean, when the heavy feeling vanishes from the deck it will *become easy to use the deck differently* for every individual.

When the same heavy low energy is present in the deck you will keep getting the low vibe with the deck when in use, restricting the flow of positivity in your readings. A positive outlook is very important for a tarot reader *as he/she has to give* it to his clients.]

Praying over your Cards

Here I will be sharing a very basic method of Praying over your Tarot cards. It will help you to explore your cards more deeply and help you to open up you to the intuitive messages that will flow through them.....

Here is a basic Prayer technique yet it is very powerful indeed and is used by experts worldwide to explore their Tarot journeys. Remember read and follow the instructions it doesn't have to be perfect, your intention to get Divine guidance to help someone with Tarot should be clear; when the technique is mastered the results will be more than satisfactory and the intuitive messages will be very accurate and precise.

** This is a very simple method that will help you draw meanings out of your tarot deck at the time when you are doing a reading. Never just cram meanings given in books or tarot sites, this is the main reason why I'm giving this technique before I share my own meanings for Tarot. Keep your Diary/Journal nearby.... Shuffle your deck by praying to help you get a card whose energy will help the most to solve the situation.

Select any one Tarot Card of your choice..... Here I have put one card randomly

Method

1. Take a card in your hand, (or choose a favourite from the whole deck to begin with). You can then do the Prayer with the other cards in descending order of your liking for them. Put the rest of the cards aside.
2. Place it in between your palms, or in the form of you on a table that isn't too high or too low, and neither too far nor too near.
3. Keep looking at the image with a constant stare, you can blink your eyes but your glance should be 100% on the card. After about 5 minutes put the card away (keep your eyes close or open, either way is perfect)
4. Now notice what you see in your mind's eye, take note of all the colours, feelings, images, poems, songs or melodies ringing in your mind, they maybe just a few words but yet sound distinct or appear clear. You

might also feel like you are watching a movie, You have to compulsorily sit even when you don't get any signs; doing this, programs your mind to give you signals the next time you set out this prayer intention. Also you can set out an intention "Whatever messages you need to know from this card, they will flow to me in next 15mins" And then stay and give yourself time for the next 15minutes to receive and intuitive messages that could come. Its not possible that you wont get anything as your intuition comes to you through your mind/ thoughts. And mind is always thinking. So once you give intention the mind will be revolving around 3-4 different sets of thoughts that might come to you again and again. Pay attention to these thoughts. And TRUST in what you get.

5. Jot down all the observances in your journal before doing anything else. This will help you to write the maximum of your intuitional messages. Write about everything you saw, smelt, felt, and tasted, during this period; Something from the external occurings might have to be noted down, while some or the internal observances might have to be noted down.

Once you are very much used to the deck images and numbering of the cards, and feelings and words seem to 'be flowing' out of you as soon as your flip cards face open you can learn that your Prayer power is now optimum and you are getting connected to the spiritual world very quickly. You may now just flip through the images once in a day to help you re-connect with every image on daily basis. This exercise is for experts who know very well every nook and corner of their deck.

Also keep in mind that you are getting connected to the Divine while praying for help, and so any lower energies cannot interfere with you. So if you are getting some negative messages try to clear out for what question the messages are flowing through that particular card. Because Tarot answers upfront. And so for questions where there are lot of things that are hidden, things start to pop out once the tarot reader asks a question when they find something critical.

[Meanings given in this book are commonly Tarot meanings, but more important and perfect meanings are what come to you for each card through your intuition. Try to build your own journal based on your intuitional messages for each card. Remember you cannot be wrong with it. Its your gut feeling.]

BEGINNING WITH TAROT

To learn Tarot and give out valuable readings you need to first know this, which is taken from Ancient Indian science about life and death which I have learnt reading from the Ramayana, some part of the Vedas, and the Puranas. It's practical and usually helps to give almost all answers to all life's problems. I have noticed that majority of religious texts give out the same morals that their people need to know. Its just jumbled up with some different stories and different names. Its just that religions were built when they felt the older one and more dominating one wasn't fulfilling their thirst for knowing THE unknown.

According to ancient Indian science every soul that is born as a Human Being has previously crossed 8400000 lives in plant & animal kingdom. After which a soul is considered as eligible to be born as a Human. The Human, being the most powerful creation of God is always born with two major Goals. First, he/she has to give something back to this planet in gratitude for all the resources that he uses on this planet while he existed(as human and all his past animal forms); as well as the **Ultimate Goal** where he has to prepare himself for his journey back to the creator. As this is the *last form* that a soul can take, humans are given the most powers which will help them to pay off all that they consume from earth; in the form of their **life's purpose** and also for their journey towards the Divine called the **Ultimate Goal.**

But the tragedy is that when a soul after being a plant and animal, going through a limited lifestyle of just hunting for food, shelter and safety from other animals as well as powers like speech that was not possible when it had the animal body, as an animal if they were beaten up or tried to get killed they couldn't voice out their complains; which now being in a human body brings this power that he/she can gather full society and tell them about his problems. This is the power of 'being human'. When these souls get to become human's they forget their life's goals and begin enjoying the 'powers' the being a human brings. And so they get into the cycle of several births and deaths, which creates tremendous Karmas itself and plus the good and bad karmas* you create while being on this planet.

*As mentioned above all good as well as bad karmas are needed to be paid off, and only after that you are eligible for Moksha; Moksha is where there is no turning back into the world of Maya and having a physical destructible body anymore. All Good as well as Bad Karmas need to be paid off. The person getting 'help' from you is loaded with debt to pay you off for that help. And you will have a future birth where you might need help and that same soul would turn up to offer help to you. Same with bad karmas, you do bad to somebody, they turn back to hurt you in your future life.

The Drama begins then. There are people who are newly born as humans as well as there are people who have gone through several cycles of births and deaths. There is a huge difference between both of these cases. We can understand this in a simple way with an example.

[The comparison is given in the form of game and life, just to make the understanding this easily.]

Every human who is newly born on this planet comes with 'no karmas tag' as well as bonus points which we can say is '100 points' (like when we play games we are offered start bonus) in order that they have a comfortable life on this planet. Now when he forgets to fulfil his life's purpose he will die without doing his duties and will have to come back as his journey is still incomplete. And when he comes back he gets a minus on his basic 100 points; let us say he will now carry 80 points. These points are helpful to go through his life smoothly, and help him overcome difficulties coming in the way of completing his life's plan and goals. So if he is feeling down, 1 point will be used from his balance and he will begin to feel good immediately.

This happens for a couple of birth and death cycles until he is left with no points. Now he will straight away go in minus. And it will be very difficult for him to feel good when even a small thing goes wrong in his life. Plus he has huge karma debt that needs to be paid off.

This is the reason why many people on this planet are very happy, like they exist on a totally different world itself. Sorrow, worries are like alien to them. Whereas on this same planet there are people who get 'down & gloomy' at the drop of a hat and find it very difficult to get out of that phase.

V.Imp - Every soul is born on this planet with certain good karmas, some bad karmas to pay off, some gifts, some lacks; and above all the soul's ultimate purpose to reach the almighty by living this life and completing his journey of births and death.

Every soul born has a life purpose that he is supposed to complete within this life. This life purpose is his contribution to this world while he lives on this planet.

The fool's journey shows this soul's journey, which we also call the fool's journey because when a soul is born in physical dimension it doesn't have any knowledge(in the sense worldly knowledge) and keeps doing mistakes and keeps falling down. As it keeps learning and living, improves itself and **rises above its folly** until it makes it so perfect that it cannot do any mistakes.

This is where it is considered complete, and perfect. That too has imperfection because it still exists in this world of Maya (World of illusion, world made up of 5 elements); the world of illusion and so it slowly leaves its body and unites with the ultimate who is perfect since past, present, and future. This unison is the actual unison where despite of being in this world it is still connected to the infinite; because of which it doesn't get shaken by negative circumstances nor gets elated by too much happiness.

The journey of the soul from beginning to completion is also the journey of soul born and completing its life's purpose and life's ultimate goal. The reason for the 'The World' card that has four different animals in four directions don't have their wings anymore, which they had during 'The Wheel of Fortune' is solely this. They have cut off all their karmic baggage (as the 'Judgment' card has appeared to justify this before. When a soul achieves its life's purpose it now is eligible to get all the good things life has; and this is now not unsteady! These pleasures are here to stay with it forever. As the ultimate Goal is achieved by this time and finding the Creator, which in itself is very fulfilling; a soul will never want anything else again in his life and be satisfied. This is depicted by the World.)

The Journey of every Soul is The Fool's Journey

Fools Journey

The Fools journey is actually every individual's journey. Tarot in this fool's journey shows how every individual is driven through certain learning phases in life and becomes a complete & enlightened soul at the end of the journey. Everybody needs to know this in life as we are actually brought up with this belief that life is always meant to be good and easy.... *But when the truths about life are learnt quickly, we suffer less.*

Also when we don't know that life has learning then we try not to change in a certain phase and then get stuck in that phase. And then we say "Life brings suffering..." but there is learning in every stage of our life and if we are aware that we have to keep learning. And if we know exactly what we have to learn then we cut out all the suffering part and make life easy for us.

This exercise can be done regularly for self-reflection and understanding and adapting to different phases of life. I usually read this fool's journey when I feel I'm surrounded by problems... and it is surprising that when I finish reading I don't find any problems with life. You can also do this for your clients.

Place the fool card in the centre and the rest of the cards around in a circular pattern according to their numbers. There are 21 cards other than the fool, with the fool numbered zero showing the beginning of the journey of the soul when everybody has to start from zero. The fool's journey is divided into three phases, childhood level, learning as an adult, and learning on a spiritual level.

Magician

The soul is born into the material world with 5 elements. The four elements lie at his table and the fifth being his spirit itself. This soul has all the creative powers of the universe to achieve success (magic) in this world. Also this card shows how every soul is filled with magic which they want to work out as soon as they begin their journey here.

The High Priestess

The high priestess shows us the hidden part of our persona, the hidden powers of the divine feminine energies that are still waiting to be tapped. The priestess sits as a guard to the spiritual world and the physical world guiding the secrets to cross it.

It is also the intuition of every soul that is ruled by the moon and is waiting to be tapped (in adults who forget this wonderful gift of God after coming to this physical world) and it works fully in the new born kids.

The Empress

The Empress is the motherly love from a mother or a guardian that a child experiences during his childhood phase. The mother loves abundantly and so this card too shows abundance in the Mother Nature that surrounds the child along with his actual mother. It's not just abundance of money but abundance of all good things that every soul needs.

The Emperor

This card shows the love of the Father that a child experiences during his childhood. The tenderness of a mother along with the authoritativeness lessons with the father. Also the control and dominance of one member of the family that keeps the child under control so that he doesn't pick up bad learning.

The Hierophant

The hierophant is the teacher and education in our world including the one from schools, gurus and our self-learning abilities. It is also the learning that happens with an individual through hardship, where he gets bad experiences.

The Lovers

A child jumps into the adolescence phase after having full blown childhood. This phase will make him more sexually aware towards himself and towards his physical needs. It also shows the time when he gets attracted to the opposite gender to start procreating in this world where continuous progress of the soul is a must by people procreating.

This is precisely the reason why everyone is gifted with the sexual force to produce kids, where new souls can be born; whose journey after past life can be continued to pay off for the remaining karmas that they have to still pay off.

The Chariot

The development of a male or female is complete is when the child is ready to face this world. He is ready to take control of himself (mind, body & spirit) and his life in his own hands.

Fool's Journey Part 2

This part of the fool's journey is for the adult fool who is now facing life. This is usually us when we complete our adolescent phase of life and step into the adult world. Now here there are certain lessons that the fool isn't aware of and has to learn. These lessons can be in any order for any individual.

Strength

In times of difficulty a soul certainly feels weak and delicate like the female strength. Female is represented in this card to show that the person is finding himself to be weak yet times are such that they have to be strong. A lion is showed handled with bare hands by this weak female which means though you feel weak you still have to face the current circumstances boldly.

Hermit

The hermit with his lantern is on a path lonely, taking one step carefully at a time. This shows that every soul passes through such a time in life when he is alone and has yet to take steps carefully based on his own instincts. The hermit has a lantern which shows him the way; this promises every soul that they will have help at hand in the form of a light that will guide them during this dark phase (the dark phase is suggested by the dark surroundings).

Wheel of Fortune

This is the wheel of fortune that is a part of everybody's life, the wheel keeps rotating and so are the phases in one's life. At one point in life when you feel you are at the top and know that your downfall is imminent, and when you fall into a pit then also remember that your rise is forthcoming. Changes are a part of life and nothing in life stays steady and so no state in life remains steady for long neither happy state nor sad state.

Justice

The tough righteous card, justice with a woman and her sword show that she is here to do justice to all. She has the scales; this is actually the justice of nature or law of karma at work. If you have good Karma then you will have good judgment passed to you, and if it's bad the woman doesn't spare anybody.

Hanged Man

This situation is also a part of life where we find ourselves in this position where we can see everything happening yet do nothing. The happenings around us are usually unpleasant ones which we cannot tolerate yet we cannot do anything because we are tied up this way.

Death

This is Practical death or death from a situation or phase in our life, where it usually is very difficult to accept and move on. But life has to move even after this and so this Death card teaches us to accept all the sudden, traumatic, abrupt changes and move on while learning from it.

Temperance

The immediate card after death showing a figure handling two cups carefully pouring liquid from one to another where he himself is balancing with one foot in water and earth.

This situation as we concur clearly from the death card shows the imbalance the death card brings into our lives, yet this card says balance your temperament which immediately comes after the death.

Fool's Journey Part 3

Fool also has to move on higher levels spiritually and so these lessons are also a must for him so that he can attain perfection. Every soul is born on this earthly plane to always keep moving forward in their spiritual journey until they achieve God-like perfection or ultimate attainment at the level of God and reuniting with Him.

Devil

The most common hindrance on the path of spirituality and evolution is the Devil, the Devil here is our inner weaknesses, bad habits, negativity that ties us up to a lower level and does not allow us to move upward. Everybody has to rise above over this devil. The Devil also represents the weak factors of a personality like anger, greed, hatred, lust, etc. which certainly brings doom for anybody who cannot win over them.

Tower

The next hindrance that comes in path of self-development, improvement and evolution of spiritually is the soul's tendency to make a secure zone where he feels he is the safest. This pic shows that there was a bolt striking at a safe place for the two people alongside their shelter that laid them bare to dangers of uncertainties. Also this shows breaking of old patterns and beliefs that don't serve their purpose anymore and develop new ones that help you better.

The Star

The star shows us a woman pouring water in two different directions, this is action showing letting go off things or people the way they want to go and not to hold them back. The water from both pots could be poured in a stream or maybe stored for selfish purposes but this person lets it go. Also water signifies the 'flow of emotions' which says don't let your negative emotions clog your system and release them for the greater good.

The Moon

The moon is the card which shows uncertainty which brings fear, the two pillars show the traveling from this world to the world of infinite which is a part of a spiritual journey but here too there could be the fear of unknown as there are infinite possibilities out there. This card says be ready for expecting the unexpected (the crab crawling out, out of the blue) and across the gates of fears.

The Sun

The sun promises a wonderful new sun 'rise' in your spiritual journey with a lot of positivity, vitality, and energy depicted by the little child hovering around his flag. Every night has a morning, every dark cloud has a silver lining, there's light at end of every tunnel which is shows in this series of major arcana; the emergence of the sun immediately after the dark period of the moon card.

Judgment

Judgment card shows there is more on the soul's development and karma side. A soul that has detached of all the comforts in this journey truthfully will get uplifted by the angel emerged above. There were ample of lessons before this card. Only when a soul has learnt them fully only then he is eligible to clear off all his karmas and move on to a higher level.

[This happens after death when judgment takes place, for the soul to move from the earthly plane to heaven. If the soul has been cut off completely from the ties of his birth then only his soul can move ahead.]

The world

This card is the successful fool, the fool who had taken a journey with carelessness is now a victory in himself, mastering his flaws, negativities and shortcomings to achieve perfection and move levels upward. Here we can see he has already succeeded and is rejoicing on completion of his life's purpose and proving worthy of being born.

Introduction to Tarot Cards

Let's move on to the explanations of the cards. There are totally 78 cards in a standard Rider-Waite pack. These 78 cards are further divided into two parts, the Major Arcana and the Minor Arcana. The word Arcana comes from Arcanum meaning "Secrets" and the major arcana means major secrets of life and minor arcana means minor secrets of life.

The tarot cards when shuffled together with the majors and the minors produce a mix and natural blend of energies corresponding to the questions of the Querent. A Querent is the one who comes to a tarot reader to ask questions, usually now we consider them as clients.

Tarot cards respond via the universal energies that are connected to us and communicate to us via the sub-conscious mind. The cards then come out accordingly and are read by the reader, the conscious mind has also studied the Tarot and so the messages are easily understood by it.

The Major Arcana begins with the Fool card which we obviously saw in the Fool's journey card. The fool is an unnumbered card which can be actually placed anywhere in the spread. The fool is like the joker card from the normal playing deck that can be placed in any position. The majors are then 21 in number and totalling to 22 with the fool card.

The Minor Arcana is further divided into 4 suits that resemble the 4 suits of the playing cards, but these cards hold a deeper meaning about the physical world rather than just numbers. These cards are just numbered in some decks (like the Thoth Tarot) but it's always good to have a pictorial representation of minors as well as it makes reading easier and these are usually found in the Rider Waite themed decks.

The four suits are the Wands, Cups, Swords and Pentacles

Wands, is a warm fiery suit, stands for Career aspect of human life

Cups, is a flowing watery suit, stands for emotional/ relationship aspect of human life

Swords, is a sharp analytical suit and stands for intellectual aspect of humans

Pentacles, is an earthy materialistic suit. This stands for physical health, materialistic life as well as money for every human.

Each suit has ten numbered cards from Aces to tens and then four court cards unlike the playing cards. Here Page is an addition. The four court cards are the Page, Knights, Queen and Kings, which are usually used as personality pointer cards or significator cards that depict people in the reading in the Querent's life or the Querent himself.

We start with meanings of each card; we begin with the major arcana and will move to minors. I request you to meditate on your cards each day. You first meditate and then go through the meaning given here; as this will allow your imagination to go wild with the meanings. If you read the meanings beforehand then you will limit yourself only to those interpretations.

I would again like to tell you that your feelings for the cards, your imagination, and what meanings you attach to the cards at the time when you read them, are most important as it is you who is reading and the cards are personally energized to you.

You must very strictly stick to what the Image tells you rather than trying to memorize the meanings given in this or any other book. This book has meanings which I feel come out of my Tarot Cards. You are free to accept these meanings if you also feel the same.

The Major Arcana

The Fool

The fool's journey showed us quite a lot about the fool, here's what I feel the fool means...

Ruled by - Element Air

Keywords- Live freely, take risks, beginnings, winding up, fresh start, travelling, taking a new adventure, trusting the universe, and be carefree towards troubles....

Appearance

The Fool is a zero numbered card which itself says it's not a card with meaning but shows the beginning, and as we saw the fool's journey in three parts it obviously shows the fool's journey. It actually shows every soul's journey that is born on this plane and the major arcana revolves around his life and its experiences.

The scene around him shows a bright sunny day which affirms that the journey of a soul begins with bright new beginnings. He has a bag with his belongings that shows he has brought his karma's good and bad ones both, which are to be paid while on this earthly plane. He is walking down a cliff that appears broken yet he isn't watchful of it, this shows the naivety of any new born soul that does not know of the upcoming dangers. The dog is walking besides him which shows he is guided by his angels.

He has a rose in his hands and is walking down as if singing a song which shows the mood of the card to be 'happy go lucky'.

Meaning

Be carefree in this world of uncertainties, you need to walk freely down your path.

Life is meant to taken as it comes as worry and panic break your flow.

The fool is seen walking down on a cliff, this gives us a feeling of fear that he may fall down. But the immediate happy feeling of the card along with the dog accompanying his side say that he is protected and has his inner guides helping him all the time.

The card numbered zero points out to phases in life when a person comes down to a zero and has to make a fresh start. The phase can be just anything; it can be a birth of a new soul, ending of a certain phase like finishing studies and moving on in search of a career, ending of relationship and beginning a new journey in search for a better relationship with the 'experiences' tied up in a bundle as lessons, or just any other phase that completed.

The journey is unpredictable yet the fool takes it in a joyful spirit and takes life as it comes. His smile and happy poise show that he is very much affirmative about the positive outcome of his journey. He is seen treading carelessly on his path which seems broken ahead. This can only be seen from a higher perspective from where we are at a point where the fool cannot see it, yet he is so much happy walking on the unknown path.

When it appears in your reading it also means that fearlessness, adventure, a spirit of carefreeness needs to be developed. Life is meant to be lived freely and fully, nobody can live their life freely if they are bounded by fear or any other negativity that blocks the flow of their life.

His naivety is seen in his head perched in heaven and feet about to slip off the road, which shows the innocence and ignorance of a soul on a path that he has never trudged before. But life is full of such roads where we all have to travel for the first time at some time or the other.

Reversed

Reversed meanings of fool says that you may be too careless in taking adventurers and risks that you are probably at the verge of loss and are likely to lose more. Risk taking is done with great care and once you get experience of it you never walk that path, but here the fool shows complete folly of walking the same path that might have led to your downfall.

The fool has innocence, but the reverse may show that you have overcome that state yet you try to use it cunningly out of wits.

Be aware of the dangers coming ahead in your path. The path you are on isn't safe. You need to 'take a look before you leap'. Purposely giving a close-eyed look to life isn't going to make life give you less trouble. You need to learn from your mistakes and not create new ones.

It may not be the right time to pack your bags and move on. You still have something that needs to be done. There is still some learning left from this situation. Don't run away from this state or your lessons would be half learnt and you might have to come back to learn them.

The Magician

Ruled by - Mercury

Keywords

Creating magic with your abilities, working out one's full potential, career of your choice, and using your talents to create magic.

Appearance

Appearance of the Magician is like a person already out with his tools and implements set up on the table and creating magic. Here the magic refers to the magic that the infinite can create through you as the magician has the infinity sign above his head. The magician has all the four suits on his table meaning that he has all the four elements that he can use to create magic and his spiritual infinite powers to bring into existence something as a product of his talents. He wears a garb and his belt is the snake that eats its own tail that again is the sign of an infinite circle. His hand points upward in the skies as if he is pointing out to us the energies of the heavens and that he can bring on earth these energies via his abilities.

The Universe promises a full supply of resources, talents, abilities and energy when you are doing the right thing/purpose of your life. The same applies to the opposite when you are not on the right path. Wealth and resources will go short and also you will lack in abilities on the wrong path. So follow your will, follow your tunes you can only sing songs that universe has made you eligible to.

Meaning

The magician means you have all the talents, abilities and resources that you need to start working. The card also shows a magician that depicts that you are the magician in your own life to help you create magic out of your own potential, the same potential that is a part of the creator's infinite energy. A creation of a dream life has begun or you have the potential and opportunities to make your life a dream life.

A new career beginning is predicted with this card as the magician has just changed from the fool. The card also shows that in the new career, new opportunities to make your desires come to fruition will be coming your way.

It's a card of taking life into your control and creating a dream life out of it. You have chances to make your life extraordinary and you have all the resources and energy for it. It also says that your energy should be focused on your goals completely right now rather than scattering them in all directions. The goals that carve your dream life are to be worked upon and given 100% attention right now. Remove all distractions aside.

Reverse

The lack of ability or resources may be giving you a feeling of being cheated by the universal energies. This happens only when you are at the wrong place or have the wrong task at hand. The task at hand is not worth applying your effort or it may not be a part of your life's purpose to fulfil it.

Distractions from your work, you may be investing too much energy in non-productive activities that are not going to be fructified in future. Neither will they bring you any good.

Reversed Magician also shows a feeling of power going unused in current circumstances. You may feel this way or it is actually happening to you yet you don't want to accept it and get out of the situation. Perhaps the magician in you has become an introvert and is lying in a dormant position just because you are not allowing him to come out; maybe this time you are busy being confused, worrying, and stressing over the fact that the magician in others around you is working. You feel stressed to bring him out. Maybe laziness is toiling in you. Or you have chosen the path of being passive and curse life rather than taking charge of life and turn it into a blessing.

The High Priestess

Ruled by - The moon

Keywords - Intuition, inner-guidance, trust yourself

Element

The high priestess is shown seated; she wears a white robe that has pomegranates on it. There are two pillars on both her sides, one is black and one is white. She is holding a scroll Torah in her hands which is half hidden and half revealed which represents the exoteric and esoteric knowledge. Her seating is calm and the moon lies at her feet representing the calm and peaceful energies of the moon at her disposal. She masters the moon energies, the cooler side of us or the intuitional side. She also represents the female guardian that is powered by moon energies.

She is sitting in between the two pillars as if she is guarding the secrets that lie within the realm. She has two pillars next to her black and white that represent the yin and yang energies. The pillars are straight and steady when both these factors are balanced only then you can enter the inner world, else the pillars would not allow you to see anyway between them.

The tapestry hung in between the pillars shuts the inner world from stray lookers. You only can enter there when you want to really go deep inside your inner world.

Meaning

Life is never always telling out your thoughts to people, its sometimes keeping secrets too. Not that telling out may prove dangerous but sometimes people don't want to know as they don't need that knowledge. She's the one who guards the unconscious mind and sits at the entrance of the gateway. She is a wealth of intuitional powers, wisdom, serenity, and calm that she bestows her permission to enter the gateway only to those who possess these qualities. When you find her in your reading remember all secrets or intuitive knowledge isn't meant to be shared. Keep your intuitional and spiritual experiences a secret. You inner world is different from others and so your messages aren't going to help anyone. They are just meant for you and are sent to you in an exclusive manner.

You have to rest for a while and wait for more knowledge to be revealed, or shown to you in the form of directions and opportunities to go forward in life.

Inner reflection is needed, connect to your inner-self which we also call higher self, that's wiser and more advanced then you. When no solution is found in the outer world then the inner world is your sure shot rescue. You may require developing your connection with this guide to get help and advice. Or you may already be getting inner guidance from the high priestess which you aren't putting into practice.

Reversed

When reversed the high priestess means you are not listening to the messages from your inner guides. You need to tune in to them as they can surely be helpful to you. The high priestess is the divine guidance within us which we can rely upon, when trusted in her she can help you develop your psychic abilities to a great extent.

You might be trying to quieten the inner voice that is trying to guide you or restrict you from doing something, but remember the inner guide once awakened can never be shut down again. This is actually a boon to us, but there are certain choices in our lives that sometimes appear good or tempting but aren't worth making. This may be the time when you are choosing such a thing which your inner guide is restricting you to choose. Listen to her!

Furthermore, this card appears when you to think others opinions are more worthy rather than your own, the priestess asks you to trust your opinions and decisions in life. When we depend completely on our inner guidance it is then that we are never let down by it. And will have a satisfactory life as we ourselves chose whatever will come.

Also there maybe things kept secret from you that you need to know, even in this situation you can ask your inner guide to help you to point out as to what those secrets are. You may also be having this habit of giving important information to people, beware if this card is negative! You should keep this info secret.

The Empress

Ruled by- Venus

Keywords- abundance of resources, femininity, motherhood

Appearance

The card appears with a female clearly meaning it's based on femininity or celebrating your feminine energies. She is seen seated lavishly on a velvet covered seat with supporting cushions, which points out the luxurious life she is having and also about her comforting nature. She wears a gown printed with pomegranates which signifies the fertility of the empress.

She is seen wearing a crown topped with stars. Her surroundings show a field ready to be harvested with abundant crops... She has a stream of water flowing at her right side. The entire theme of the card is of luxuries of the materialistic world. We can also call this card a Nature card with Mother Nature or mother earth seated amongst abundance. Natural wealth comes in when nature is satisfied by the conduct of the beings she's around; this is the feeling reflecting from the Empresses face. Her look says she can easily obtain whatever she wants.

There is a golden aura shown around her crown region which shows she has developed her spiritual side too, her energies are pure and generated by her good heart and spirit. She is with abundance yet her aura reflects the golden being that she is within. The card is for being deeply grounded even after attaining riches.

Meaning

The basic feel of this card is for the feminine energy it brings, the feminine energy to care, nurture, love, bring harmony, give birth all are different sides of this feminine card. You need to balance out your feminine energies and give yourself credit to be born as a female. If you are a male then you need to develop the qualities of the empress like caring and nurturing. The female side of our person is also the side of creativity inherent within us. Develop your creative interests and give them time and space to expand.

The empress as the name suggests is the bringer of abundance, in a usually materialistic world. She is seen seated lavishly on a very luxurious seat with lot of support which shows you have people around you to support you along with material stability. If you don't have such people know that this card brings you a message of forthcoming support.

Empress shows actual birth or pregnancy, depends on cards along that fall after this. Or this may show birth of new ideas or creating opportunities. This card also sends you the message from mother Earth to get into natural environment or to start eating naturally available organic food. Try to be in natural surroundings and let nature cleanse your energies with its 5 natural healers the earth, fire, air, water and your spirit itself. When we connect with nature our body automatically starts healing itself, such are the healing abilities of our magnificent planet.

Also the calm poise with which she raises the wand in her hand shows that the abundance around her is earned through her efforts. Her creativity has helped her get to this much abundance. The motherly feel of this card may also point out to some people in your life who are acting as your mother!

Reverse

The reverse card says you might be suppressing, cursing, or disregarding your femininity or creative energy, which may be resulting in lack of abundance or resources.

On the other side you might have disrupted your natural energy balance to a great extent resulting in disharmony or even ill-health. If you are not experiencing this then your lifestyle and food choices maybe such that may lead you to this place in future. Being too much off the path of one's own spirituality or of ones life's purpose leads us to this position; where you hardly find any resources and satisfaction. See for the cards ahead of this to provide the solution of getting out of this situation.

You may be using your motherly side to over-do things. The people who never seem satisfied by your emotions maybe just consuming you energies this way. Remember feminine energy is creative energy; use this creativity to help people bring out the best in them rather than just vaguely trying to satisfy their egos.

It may also revolve around issues related to femininity, pregnancy or periods. Any disharmony in these processes show the undernourished female in you tugged deep inside and wanting to come out.

The Emperor

Ruled by- Aries

Keywords- Dominance, power, ruler, leadership, fatherhood, law and order

Appearance

The appearance of the emperor as the name suggests he is seated on a throne with hand supports of rams, this is the symbol for Aries and so this card carries Aries' energy. The emperor is wearing a cloak that appears royal showing his dignified position in society and a crown on his head symbolizing his power and wealth. He is shown wearing his iron suit beneath his kingly clothes which isn't noticed at first sight but it's still there signifying that he is protected from within by his inner strength and the strength of the ram, and outwardly appears with normal clothes. He is benevolent with the good and ready and well-protected if bad comes his way.

He is the masculine energy following the empress, he has the symbol of ankh in his right hand that is the Egyptian symbol of life and its observer, and on his left has the symbol of a globe which says he rules the earth, this may also signify that he rules the world he is in; comprised of his family or if we see it from a greater point of view, he rules over his mind, body and soul.

Meaning

The card which holds masculine energy first of all points out to a fatherly figure in your life or somebody in charge or head of the family or head of some department who holds control or needs to be taken permission of. He maybe a stern or strict person who is capable for being a ruler/leader. He is always strong from within but appears calm from above.

The Fool in the fool's journey has the Emperor as his Father. He provides the warmth, strength, security and confidence to face the world to the fool. The mother is responsible for the child's development emotionally whereas the father helps the child to be ready to face the world and make him self-confident in his abilities.

This is also a card of grounding of male energy in the physical plane. The emperor brings stability to the desires of the empress. He rules and makes sure everyone under his rule is happy and satisfied. He is the one in charge and so always wants things done in a proper manner. He ensures law and order for his people.

The emperor is very good in a leading role, a manager, an in-charge, admin, where he can use his energy to the fullest. He has fiery energy in him to make things happen correctly which is signified by the reddish-orange colour of his background. He can be in charge, care, protect and at times when he needs to, fight for his people where too he would give his best as people trust him for his role.

Reversed

The reversed emperor is the misuse of the powers of the emperor, tyranny or dominance to the people who are below him, or who trust him. This dominance can be from you or anyone around you at your workplace or family; or seeing it from a deeper point of view the rigidness of certain beliefs that don't serve your purpose anymore maybe dominating your mind.

This may also sometimes signify the change of authoritative figure around workplace, or a temporary substitute for it. The current in-charge may no longer be as worthy as he used to be before, and it's time to change the boss.

This card when reversed in a relationship or family reading shows an authoritative figure who's too dominating trying to subdue the voice of others; you may possibly have such a person in your environment who casts a shadow on your abilities due to his dominance.

It shows lack of passion or a lackadaisical attitude towards your duties. The true spirit of your post may be missing.

The Hierophant

Ruled by- Taurus

Keywords- studying, teaching, getting a guru, learning, education, spiritual wisdom/ spiritually wise person

Appearance

The Hierophant is a pope like figure who is seated in a holy place looking like a church; he is shown giving knowledge or teaching people sitting in front of him. There are two pillars like the one found behind the priestess, and there lie the keys at the feet of this figure; which signifies that the hierophant has the keys to enter the inner world. The priestess was sitting in the way and there was a tapestry hiding the inner world's secrets but here the theme of the card says that there is already the need to tap into the knowledge of the inner world due to which the hierophant has appeared. He is here to help you find the keys to enter into the inner world.

He has the keys to go to the inner world, or the solution to your problems, or adds knowledge that you lack, which is shown by the teaching spirit of the card. He wears a crown on his head that suggests the high levels of spirituality that he has reached. His hand has a triple cross, again a sign of holiness and hope. His fingers point out upwards showing that he is asking you to trust in the higher energies or even bringing the knowledge from the higher realms.

Meaning

The card means that in this world of learning the fool needs a teacher to help him understand life and how to handle it just like the old-fashioned principle to send the child to a guru before he is ready to face the world is important. The teaching will help the child to grow into a stronger human being and help him deal with day-by-day difficulties of life.

This may also mean that you need to add some more knowledge to your existing knowledge base. You may need to learn something to add to your expertise. You can either do this by finding someone who can teach this to you or you yourself could learn to attain mastery.

The card may also point towards the inner learning of lessons by oneself, life sometimes leads you to difficult ways and doesn't leave you choices to take help from someone at this time know that you will have to be your own guide or your own teacher to help you move further in life.

It may show the need to take help from some counsellor, teacher, or guru who is recognised in their field. It may also show your ability to be such a person who can guide others to have an easy life either a counselling type of work or a tutor in the field you are.

Reverse

The reverse of hierophant shows that you may not trust yourself and always let others influence you. This won't help you as the knowledge that you have is correct or the knowledge that can come from your genius would prove to be beneficial to you.

Additionally, there may be someone who may be misleading you in your path by their treachery so you need to move away from such people.

Your self-trust or self-confidence would be led down so much that you don't trust yourself and as a result you cannot trust others too. Otherwise life's lessons might be so tough that you might have made grave mistakes which makes you doubt your decisions too much and you fear trusting yourself. The lessons from life are only to make your faith in yourself more strong. You don't have to go weak but get more and more decisive and alert while deciding.

The Lovers

Ruled by - Gemini

Keywords - Love, romance, dreams come true, follow your heart

Appearance

This card appears with two figures male and female looking at each other, they are nude and the entire scene of pic shows that they are lovers eternal soul mates meant for each other and have met today. There is a huge angel in the background with large spread wings giving a message that God or the Angels have made this relationship happen and they will protect and nurture the love of the Lovers. There is a tree in the background of the female with ripe fruits showing her fertility aspect at the same time has a serpent coiled on the trunk warning the male not to get too much attracted to the Maya inducing beauty. The male too has a tree in background that shows it's on fire showing the passionate desire of man.

The sun shines brightly above the two of them, shows the brightness and positive energy coming into their life through their relationship. The light also appears like a blast through which the angel has appeared giving us a sign of a miracle happening out of the blue.

The cloud in between shows the angel coming out of nowhere, which shows how life is very uncertain and unpredictable and that miracles happen at every step in our lives.

Meaning

The lovers card as the pic shows first of all suggests that there romance may soon enter your life; if you are a male then you will find a potential female or if you are a female you will find your man of your dreams soon. If the question is regarding an existing relationship then know for sure that this card signifies that the lovers are soul mates and its an eternal couple bonded by angels or eternal couple bonded from heaven met on earth.

This card not only shows a romantic relationship but also loving and affectionate relationship with friends or with some members of the family.

The relationship that is signified by the Lovers is notified in the following cards that are in the reading after the lovers. There may be any court cards or any major arcana card that may signify a person in the Querent's life. The love and affection followed by the Lovers card is eternal the relationship that is being talked about is of course a Loving one and also a gift of the Angels which cannot fade. See for necessary clues to maintain the relationship in cards ahead of this.

This card may also show self-love developing, perhaps you might be in love with yourself as life is getting easy or you are doing things your heart suggests. Pamper yourself and your body with things you like, give yourself a nice treat or a visit to a parlour or a meditation retreat to nurture your soul.

This lover's card can also indicate love for your career or your dream job that has just been fulfilled. When this appears in a career spread then the Querent's dream career is on his way, or maybe the cards might be telling him to choose a path that is dear to him.

Reverse

The Lovers reversed shows that there might be problems in the relationship, either one of the partners may be cheating or the relationship is on the verge of breaking. It may also show problems in relationships other than that of lovers; friendships, family, relationships at office, or with relatives which have been going sour for some time. The outcome or solution may be shown in following cards after this card.

The reverse of Lovers is anything that goes against your heart, you may be engulfed in life where it is not getting easy, getting love-less or perhaps you are not on the right path.

Career wise this card may sound tough, you may not get work of your choice for some time or maybe before you get your dream job you would need to pass through this undesirable profession due to some reasons. You may feel you are stuck in the wrong job or people in the workplace might be difficult that may make you hate your workplace.

The lovers card may on a deeper level signify that the love for one's self needs to be developed, there are many times in our lives that are tough and when we create mistakes, or our actions are such where we are humiliated when we usually start hating ourselves. The more intense the circumstance the more we develop hatred, embarrassment guilt etc. feelings towards ourselves. Life then starts getting difficult when one doesn't Love oneself; this card maybe pointing to you to develop "self-love" now as this will enable the path of life to be filled with love.

The Chariot

Keywords - Taking charge, balancing negative and positive polarities, taking control of one's life

Ruled - cancer

Appearance

The chariot appears with a man standing on a chariot, there are two figures that look dressed in Egyptian style, one is black and one is white which shows our negative and positive side. The man in the chariot looks very confident, he wears his armour and looks "ready" for the fight; the fool here is ready to fight with the ups and downs of life signified by the black and white figures. He is in control of his negative and positive attributes and can now face life bravely.

The crown of the charioteer has a star which shows his connection to his own spiritual side or his spiritual side guiding his life like a spirit guide. There are wings on the front of the chariot showing that wherever that chariot goes it will be guided by the angels. It also brings a sense of trust in the process of life that though it is uncertain our angels and guides make sure we tread our paths safely.

Meaning

The Fool has now become a grownup and has now finished schooling; he is ready to set foot into the open world. Here he needs to take care of his positive and negative attitude as he is alone on this journey. Only when the two anima's are balanced his chariot can move steadily; if either one of them dislocates or gets imbalanced then his chariot of life would wobble and he would fall down.

This card means the time to take a leap forward in life has come, you need to be patient, confident, daring in the face of fears and self-reliant to the extent that you are in control of your life and have to be the strongest, toughest and the most dependable person for yourself.

Take charge in your life, take charge of all good things as well as the mistakes you might have made in your life. The time to get weak is over, you have to be bold and take the move to lead your life solely by yourself. Your inner guides both of male persona and the female persona are helping you balance your mind. The high priestess and hierophant are now within you and guiding your life's path being the two figures connected to your chariot.

You may be leading a disorganized life and this cards popping up in your reading says you have to balance your good and bad and get up and get going in your life.

Reverse

Reversed chariot shows that the fool wasn't balancing his persona well, either the positive or the negative aspect of his personality got imbalanced and his chariot fell off. You need to balance your mind and don't let negativity cloud your consciousness. To live a steady happy life you need to keep moving despite the circumstances.

You don't want to take charge of your life, the uncertainties of life are weighing you down and instead of getting confident you are freaking out by the day-by-day turmoil life brings. Perhaps you are only concentrating on the negative aspects. You need to shift your focus on the good things in yourself, your life, and the people around you.

Also when this card turns up reversed in a reading it may show that you have some task to complete in the current place and only then you can move on. No running away from your responsibilities. A rash paced life will make you regret in future the things you missed on the way. Life never wants us to move rapidly through it. It wants us to enjoy every step we take to walk on this beautiful planet for that is what creation is. A human is born as the best creation and ought to feel thankful for all the miracles around him.

The Strength

Ruled by- Leo

Keywords- Control, bravery, stamina, dare

Appearance

The appearance of Strength card shows a lady dressed in a robe with a tiara on her head, she tries to open the mouth of a lion that in unchained with her bare hands. She has a sign of infinity over her head signifying her strength coming from the universe.

She wears a flowery belt that signifies the natural freshness in her attitude in spite of her strong abilities. A female is usually delicate and is associated to weakness among the genders but here the female is shown holding an unchained lion which itself is a very brave deed. A lion is very difficult to hold on even for the bravest and strongest of men, but here the lion is shown calmly standing next to this woman and not just that the female tries to open the mouth of the lion with her bare hands. The lion is unchained which itself shows how dangerous it can be to handle that creature but she also tries to pull open its mouth with her bare hands. Her attire shows she does not have any weapons that might help her if the lion attacks her. Yet she has the daring to do such a brave act.

The lion too is shown calm and allowing the lady to open her mouth.

Meaning

The Fool that was a child and an immature soul till now (in the first phase) is a grown up, and the first lesson life gives him is that of Strength. Life would bring a lot of problems as mighty and deadly as the Lion but the Fool has the strength to handle them. This fool is each and every soul who is on this planet. And every fool will have the strength to conquer his problems. As this is the first lesson of life for every soul who sets foot in the outer world once grown up.

The card suggests strength in the face of hard times. You have to be strong if you were facing troubled times or situations that make you weak. The circumstances may appear to be tough and unconquerable yet they are "tame-able". You just need to increase your willpower.

The situation though appears tough is tameable, the problem will readily give up in front of you. You only need to take action or a brave step forward to handle it.

She has the infinity symbol above her head meaning that she has this strength coming down from infinity. Your problems would appear very difficult to anyone who hears about them but the infinity symbol shows that you will be able to handle them on your own.

This also means that when you face a problem tough and difficult to handle like the ferocious Lion, give it gentleness and affection like a female can give and that the toughest of people/problems can be handled with ease.

Also this card may signify the beast within you which either comes out at difficult times like the anger or bout of depression which may not allow thinking or acting in the correct manner. The Strength card says to manage this beast with compassion and gentleness. We never want our weaknesses to magnify, and they magnify only when treated with harshness. So Strength says treat your beast with compassion and you will surely win over it.

Reversed

The strength reversed shows that circumstances or outer forces which would overpower and overwhelm you, you may feel weak and defeated in the war of life. Also it may feel that life is out of control, the outer difficult circumstances seem to be more powerful than they are. This only shows that you have lost touch with your inner willpower. You have allowed the outer world to overpower you to such an extent that you now doubt whether anything more powerful than that does exist or not.

In career reading it signifies that you are driven by the outer world, you may find the views or opinions of your friends more powerful than your own and so you feel driven to the careers they like or suggest. Also if not forcefully driven by people then you may yourself be wavering as you are unsure of what to select. Your lack of confidence may take you to the wrong places.

In in a family or relationship reading, this card may tell that people around you or your partner may overpower you. They may be dominating to an extent bringing fear in you before doing anything on your own. This too is because you have given away too much of your control to them. They feel that you might have done that because you are not much confident about yourself and want them to take your decisions for you. And so they consider it their duty to command and control you. Also their showing power, might have accidentally given you a reaction of "Oh I'm so scared" there is the law of nature that applies here; the more scared you are of something the more things/people would come to you to increase your scaring quotient. This situation will continue untill you discover your inner strength and take responsibility for yourself.

The Hermit

Ruled by - Virgo

Keywords- Inner reflections, loneliness, step after introspecting carefully, continue moving ahead...

Appearance

The Hermit appears to be wearing a long robe; he has a white beard suggesting he is quite aged. He has a lantern to lighten his path, and the environment around him is dark. There is nightfall and he seems to be going somewhere alone, the path where he is walking looks uneven pointing out to impending dangers and so he is walking inspecting the path carefully.

The Hermit is the Fool's second lesson in this world, the path being lonely plus the age and weak body of the hermit yet doesn't have to stop if the circumstances aren't ideal. His posture shows that he is walking which signifies that life should continue at any point of time. Don't stop while darkness prevails. Looking back would only scare you as you'll see your problems becoming bigger than they are (signified by a shadow if you would look back in darkness), but walk in the direction of the light.

Meaning

The Hermit when turns up in your reading means you have to walk carefully on your path, don't stop even if you are alone. You have the light in your hands to guide you and a staff to protect and help you tread the uneven path. Life's roads are always not smooth and we feel we need support (usually emotional and moral support) from people, but even when you don't get it you still keep going. You have to support yourself in these situations.

The path that you have chosen would require walking down carefully, no panicking or running back. You may find it difficult and yet the path promises that there would surely be good returns in return of this pain of walking down the difficulties. The Hermit also tells us about time in life when we don't need to depend on others and introspect with oneself knowing that life's answers lie within us.

Your path of life however it is still yours, it reminds me of the phrase "We come alone on this planet and go alone from this planet", the card's energy wants to remind you of this truth of life. When we are born we have all the knowledge how our life is going to be, and how we are spiritually evolved to solve the problems of life. The materialistic world engulfs you so deep into attachment that this answer disappears somewhere. Then there come difficulties in your life and the foundation of your being shakes to such an extent that this answer surfaces up in your mind. The Hermit will turn up in your reading if there is such a time going on in your life.

You might need this time of solace to find your life's purpose.

Reversed

The reversed Hermit is showing that you have taken too much of solace in your life, or you might have been cut off from the world so much that the world may not seem to know that you even exist in it. This time is when you have to go and mix around with people. Too much of inner involvement or spiritual journey will leave you ungrounded leaving you feeling "out of the world".

A Hermit reversed can also show that thc Querent would be trying to act as an extrovert and mix and mingle around with people, talk, laugh loudly etc. just to show his presence; but deep inside the Hermit would still be disconnected and may be trying to find a connection this way.

The Hermit may be on a difficult path that was uneven, when reversed this card shows that the Hermit is now on a good path that eases a lot of his concerns. He may no more be in any need inner reflection, such a time may be over and he now needs to stop being overzealous and reflective.

Also this card reversed shows that you may be lacking wisdom, or maybe trying to act foolish on purpose.

The Wheel of Fortune

Ruled by- Jupiter (The biggest of all planets, shows the power of this card)
Keywords- Turn of time wheel, change in fortune, drastic changes

Appearance

The Wheel of Fortune shows a wheel where there is a figure shown on top, the other is on the left which is falling down, and the one on the right is rising. There are four figures in all four directions, there's an angel on the top-left, an eagle on top right, a bull on bottom left, and a lion on the bottom right; the bull is for Taurus sign, the lion is for Leo, eagle is for Scorpio and the angel is for Aquarius. The fact that they have wings suggests that this card's prediction may vary each time due to the constant movement of stars, and their shift would have a different impact on all signs.

Also this card helps us believe in the uncertainty of the planetary movements and its effect on us. As these movements can change the path at any time too much dependence on it for one's fortune isn't ideal.

The wheel in the centre has the letters T, A, R, O, which when read in a full circle would make TAROT. Also when we read it anticlockwise it becomes the Torah the book/scroll that the High Priestess was holding which was to be kept secret.

Meaning

The "Tora" seems to be revealed in here which was hidden during the childhood or the developing phase of the Fool, the Torah has secrets about the laws of life. The uncertainty of life is one of the biggest secrets that are contained in that book that is revealed here. The Fool that was learning tough lessons of life now has bumped in one tougher lesson of life "Life is never constant".

This card shows great change, good as well as bad. It depends on the Querent's current condition. If the Querent is on high skies then it may be time for a downfall, if this question is related to a particular "stuck" situation than this card brings relief indicating that there will be a change soon.

This card rather than indicating physical changes is an indicator of shifts in ego. When one is flying in high skies then they have to fall down, also when one is emotionally low will quickly soar to great heights of happiness. The centre to the wheel is always steady it never rises or falls, but when we try to be on the top of the wheel then the changes of movement of the wheel are going to affect us. The idea of this card is also to give a message is that to try to get out of the high-low cycle or good and bad part that life gives. If you wish for good you will surely have to face the bad too sooner or later. But when you stop falling into this race of negative and positive then you actually become centred and then the wheel starts moving according to your will.

The good and bad are the ones that take your life out of your control, when you get out of the cycle of it you actually create your own future.

The turning of the Wheel of Fortune is also not unjust, the centre has the wisdom from the Torah which says that the wheels have turned and brought bad fortune just because you are not on the right track. You are not walking according to your heart's desire. Figure out the thing that you are doing "out of will" and you'll soon recognise why nature has tilted the wheel to put you down. While the wheel shows that there are times good and bad you can make the turning of the wheel quick by quickly adapting to your life's path and do what your heart says.

Reversed

The reversed Wheel of Fortune shows that you are not bound to any external force in our life to bring changes; you are completely under your control. Also this card turning up may say that you are not flexible to changes, you have formed so rigid patterns of living in all areas that it may be getting difficult to deal with you at times. Nature is changing and as you are a part of nature you have to accept this quality of Mother Nature. When you don't accept it Nature takes hold of you and makes the change by force and then you would feel devastated.

This card may also signify that there is an unreasonable waiting period in your life. There is a wait in bringing the change you want to happen. The results that you are waiting for may take time unknown or any work or task expected to complete and deliver results will seem to be delayed.

Also when this card comes up, there are four astrological signs in each corner which when reversed may mean that your astrological chart might be having more stars that are going through a transit and so you might feel a bit uncomfortable with yourself or your life may seem to take drastic changes in a random manner raising stress.

Justice

Ruled by- Libra

Keywords- Justice, nature's justice, law, principles

Appearance

The justice card appears with a female sitting with a stern look; she has the scales to bring balance to life along with a Sword in her right hand. The perfect card to appear after the Wheel of Fortune, the one who was not good in any way, was enjoying life and its resources till now which has now come down and the Justice of the divine is passed to give him his punishment.

Also as it is for good people, a good person toiling hard as yet getting slow success gets a much needed change in fortune with the Wheel of Fortune and soars up to the heights of unimagined success that the Divine Justice now bestows him with the sweet fruits of his hard work.

The Fool has to pass through this Justice card in his life many times, for getting the results of his good and bad deeds. Once in life the Justice hits too hard to make the Fool remember its consequences just so that he won't dare to do all that wrong again.

The pillars and the tapestry covered between them show that the Fool hasn't yet tried to venture into this inner world which is full of wisdom. The idea behind it is that till a man doesn't start knowing the God within him he keeps doing wrong/right deeds without having any idea of what he is doing. When one travels into the depths of one's soul the secret to the creation of this cosmos is revealed which then helps the Fool, who by then wouldn't be a fool anymore, to evolve and get out of the good/bad deed cycle.

Meaning

The meaning of this card is clear by the very keyword printed on it, the wrong would be punished and the right ones will flourish. From a straightforward point of view it means the injustice or the slow pace that your life had till now which might have proven an obstacle in your path is now going to be put right by the forces of nature. The Wheel of fortune has turned and the Justice for all your hard work is going to start getting repaid to you.

Also the scales show that there is going to be balance in your life, if your life in imbalanced in any area know this for sure that justice will be served. This card also may turn up in your reading as a warning to you if you are being dishonest in any way to the outer world or to yourself. Justice asks you to do justice to yourself, only then the outer world will do justice towards you.

Justice brings law and order, truth, honesty, harmony, balance into our world. Justice by the Infinite intelligence always keeps balance in this world and cutting away all that negates this card's true essence. The Fool here learns to be true to himself as well as towards the world. Also if the Fool was being tested unjustly then this card helps him to bring faith in the higher Justice.

Justice card in a career reading means to be truthful and honest at the workplace, also the cards lying on both the sides of this card do matter. Also if it's in the career reading it would point out towards the working environment that may indicate strictly following law and order and honesty, being the first virtue.

This card turning up in relationship will ask you to be true to your feelings, sometimes people try to please their partners and overdo it even when they don't feel like doing it. They feel that they must give their full all the time to the relationship in order to keep the relationship going. But human nature is always different; it cannot be stable or steady. So respect your feelings and be true to them. If you feel drawn towards someone then this may be the time to accept it. You have to first accept it as your mind might be getting disoriented due to nonacceptance.

If the question is about legal issues it says that the result would be in the Querent's favour, also check other cards in the spread.

Reversed

The reversed Justice shows dishonesty, disruption of law and order, lies, imbalance. This state would be of the outer world of the Querent or the inner state where he would be dishonest with his own feelings or towards others. There may also be the same response from the outer environment towards him.

The Justice card may also show the imbalance in the Querent's life, which may be due to his untruthfulness of dishonesty in the past. His past acts might now be biting him back as a result of his karma. There may be time of suffering due to it. But the law of karma states that there is no other solution to it other than paying off the debt.

In a relationship reading this may show dishonesty or cheating towards one's partner. The one who is asking the question may be doing this or their partner would be dishonest towards them. Also see the position where this card falls as this act of disloyalty would be either in the past or might still happen in the future. There may be also a possibility that the in Querent's family there is some treachery going on or cheating going on towards the Querent or towards other member such that this might be affecting the total balance of the family.

In legal issues if this turns out reversed than it might show a defeated case. Also it might show unusual delays for the verdict to be passed. The cards following this card will clarify that.

The Hanged Man

Ruled by - Neptune

Keywords- Limbo period, wait and watch, trapped feeling, look things differently

Appearance

The Hanged man is shows hanged upside down tied to a branch of a tree. He is also tied up further by hands and legs showing his helplessness in the situation.

The tree is shown with fresh leaves growing, showing that life isn't stopping here; growth continues. It also signifies that the environment around him is growing and he is the only one arrested this way.

There is a golden halo around the hanged man's head which shows that at this time too he is filled with positivity. Perhaps this is a learning time for him to accept growth and success for environment around him too. Other feelings associated with this card are patience, letting go, go with the flow, learning from things around you etc. It also shows spiritual advancement in the phase when materialistic progress is shunned (signified by the physical body)

Meaning

There is time for being patient and calming down the rush that you were in till now. Also it may show that acting in the current situation isn't favourable and a wait and watch period follows. You may find the outer environment overpowering you. The only message that comes for you in this situation is "letting go". There may be lessons of waiting, letting go, patience, and gathering wisdom from the present for you.

The physical body is suspended but the golden halo still shines which means that your physical world may not be much progressing but this is the perfect time for you to develop yourself spiritually.

Also being selfless or and giving your benefits and time is suggested here for the ones around you. Your nature maybe too hasty or hyper and this circumstance might be very difficult for you to digest. But when life has brought to this day it surely wants you to learn to be more patient in your work and maintain a calm composure.

The time may not be right for you as you are not able to control your surroundings and yourself too. People maybe controlling you or you might have been giving too much of yourself to others that they have finally placed you in a position where you cannot take any decision for yourself. You need to check other cards along in this reading if it says to be in this state then fine but if there is an action card next to this card then you must not stay in this position for long. Let loose yourself and start moving in your desired direction.

In a relationship reading you might find being dominated of letting go too much of yourself. Being patient and calm is your first key to this situation. Also see other cards in the spread if they suggest that the partner is too bossy then you need to take control in your hands.

Career reading shows you don't know where you career is heading and your inability to take it in a particular direction; trust the higher intelligence they know what's better for us more than us and be assured that you would be headed in the right direction.

Reversed

Reversed hanged man shows the man in his normal position which shows that he is neither suspended anymore, he might be free from the bondage or the setting back thoughts of his own mind now and is free to move around the world. Also it might show that there is nothing to let go and accept defeat or being tied up. You are now fully in charge of your life.

The wisdom that you need will be attained by doing action; being stagnant will not help here. You have to "act" in order to bring changes into your life. To keep working or keep flowing is the way for gaining wisdom for you.

Hanged man reversed also shows that the stagnant time in your life is over the time when you felt out of control and other around you controlling you is also over you now need to move on and start living your life according you your will.

In a relationship reading it might be showing change of the views of the partner towards and taking control of him/her they might not want to give in the relationship much. Or they might want to be freer here.

Career reading maybe showing, that you are very much wise and ready and aware for taking action. The Fool that was learning while being suspended has now completed his learning and has come down from the tree and is going to move further in life.

Death

Ruled by- Scorpio

Keywords- Death, Transformation, extreme change, unacceptable changes, cleansing of old.

Appearance

The Death card as the name suggests shows literal Death in its imagery. The Death is the man on his horse we can also call him the death giver man that is described in many scriptures across the world. He has a flag in his hands and wears Armour. The Armour suggests that he is invincible and unconquerable. His horse's reign also has the signs of skull and bones imprinted on it showing its sign of entry.

There are people shown pleading for life below him, they are in royal clothing with a crown showing that they are some kings or from the kingdom. But Death is equal for everybody. There is none more important or less important to Death. After dying, everybody goes to the same world which is why the significance.

The two pillars that were at the back of the high priestess, hierophant and justice card now show a sunrise from the other side which signifies that when death takes away something from this world something new is already on its way to enter this world.

There is a boat shown that is said to take souls away from this world to other side from this world.

Meaning

The Death card shows literal death in some cases, where the health issues of the Querent or other person around him is concerned, it may also show up in absence of any health issues. The cards around the death card are to be studied properly.

Here also is death is circumstances, phases in life either good or bad usually the ones that have become old and worn out. Also the death of all that is false, unwanted from life that you might have been holding up just as you are too much attached to it or them.

The Fool has to go through this toughest test also in his life where he might have to face somebody's death, death which is the ultimate truth on this physical dimension which leads him to the urge of wanting to know about the secrets of life and will allow him to hasten his progress due to its uncertainty.

The Death card also shows renewal perhaps there's something going away from your life, something which too much attractive for you and you can't let go, but you know that it has to go. The sunrise beyond the pillars shows that there is already some replacement already on its way into your life for the thing you are parting with.

In different readings it may show the end of relationships, the end of a career, the death of a person you are close to or the end of phases that seemed to last forever. This also shows cleansing of your life energies by driving away things you don't need any more by the higher intelligence. Someone that's unconquerable, but stay assured that what is going away wasn't useful to you anymore and so it was taken away.

Death also is a cleanser, as the body that gets old and weary is destroyed and a fresh vital body is sent to the earth. It also shows that situations that were taking too much from you are ending now, some difficult time which seemed endless will end soon end which brings a fresh hope to your life. You will have to start your life anew like a soul starts life from A… B... C... i.e. like being reborn.

Reversed

The death reversed may show situations where there might be a close encounter with death and the person will be miraculously saved, it can be for the Querent or someone around him. It may also show drastic change in the health of someone who was earlier suffering to a great extent.

Also this card on the other hand shows that change which was coming has come to a halt. It shows unwanted delays, setbacks to the changes that you were expecting adding more to your frustration. Just know this that Death card is inevitable and so the change has to come now or some other time in future. But if it's brought to a halt it's done by the divine intelligence, you might have to still learn something from this situation.

There might be something that doesn't need to be brought to an end in by you. See if you are ending something abruptly, it may not need to be ended. It may show not to bring an end to relationships, career, business decisions etc.

The relationship reading may show that the relationship needs to be given time so that it does not 'die' or there may be a little time left for the relationship to end. If the relationship's end is taken to the court this reversed card may show delays in ending the relationship or delay in the court case for getting the result.

Delay is the changing of any situation which is being difficult to handle. There is a little more 'dirt' left to come out of it, so that death can clean it altogether.

Death is the ultimate cleanser; before it comes it brings out the worst in or around you; just because it can clean it fully. As more old goes out only that much new freshness can come in. So just allow things to run its course.

Temperance

Ruled by- Sagittarius

Keywords- Stay balanced at difficult times, handle delicate matters carefully, control your temperament

Appearance

The card appears with a figure standing with one foot immersed in water and other on the ground. The person has wings, though he is balancing himself on his feet which are unevenly placed. The cloak is white which is the colour for peace. There is a red triangle within a square on the chest of the person that signifies balance even in the face of chaos.

The person balances himself which is a very difficult task, and on top of it is pouring water from one container to another. The water in the container also shows careful handling of emotions. The figure is that of the angel who has a golden halo around his head which shows his ability of balance and harmony coming from his wisdom.

There is also shown a crown in the background signifying the connection of his crown chakra with the divine world.

The Fool that had faced the tumult scene of Death card which shakes the very being of a soul due to uncertainties of life has now to face Temperance immediately suggesting to bring balance to one's mind immediately after the transformation has taken place, mourning or spending too much time to understand why the change happened isn't worth it.

Meaning

The Fool now has to learn to be peaceful from inside as well as the outside. He has to learn to do so though situations may not be favourable. He still can be in full control of himself and control his life and his belongings.

The card may show that you need to calm down emotions that increase your turbidity. The angelic figure shows being in a balanced composure. The angel also asks you to balance even when the time is not such. There may be imbalance in the surroundings but still try to balance on the toppled surface and regain your composure.

Carefully handle your emotions or the emotions about the person concerned in this reading. You may be dealing with someone very delicate or sensitive. Also this may show the taking care of young ones at your home and that will bring out the angelic self in them. Teaching young children to nurture peacefulness will also help them to grow up with good conduct.

Temperance shows learn to be at peace from outside shows by the balancing of the body on one foot on ground plus also inner peace shows by the careful handling of the resources that are at your disposal right now.

Only a spiritually developed soul has adequate balance to be in a calm composure from outer and inner realms. Try connecting to your spiritual self along with the current jobs at hand. Spirituality and physical world go hand in hand as all worlds exist simultaneously.

Reversed

Reversed temperance might mean that you might not be able to balance your life. Things would be getting out of control. The surrounding environment may not allow you to take control over your inner or outer self. This may just be your belief as you have formed a habit of depending on others. This might be the right time to teach you to understand this and start to rely upon yourself.

It may also show that you need to bring your emotions under control. The emotional disruption may also point towards physical body blocks. When our emotions are not under our control they start controlling the physical body and vice versa.

You might not be using your angelic side; you may be totally disconnected with your divine self, giving rise to this situation. Tough times are actually a blessing in disguise. This time may show total lack of balance and harmony in your life but it may also push you to develop your spiritual side now.

Life brings you problems just to make changes to your inner and outer self. You will always change in times like these so life makes sure that you learn the lesson either way.

DEVIL

Ruled by- Capricorn

Keywords- Bonding, imprisonment, attachment, lust, greed

Appearance

The Devil is the third phase of the Fool's journey, where he has to develop his spiritual side for completing the cycle of life and uniting with the creator. So the first and foremost lesson on the spiritual path is the severing of attachments which the devil here is shown holding.

The Devil shows a man and a woman tied up to a pole and the pole, and on the pole sits a huge devil. The Devil is half man and half goat; which is why it is associated with the Capricorn sign. The male and the female connected to the chain have their hands loose and can free themselves from their bondage whenever they want.

The two figures have horns on their heads signifying the devilish sides of our nature. They both have tails, the female's tail has fruits at the end and the male's has fire. It feels that the devil just set the fire to the male. The fire is in form of excessive passion, lust that the man would approach the fertile female with.

The devil is shown with bat-like wings that show us the theme of darkness. The devil brings out the dark side of our nature. He has huge horns like the horns of the goat. And his expression shows that he is in control of the two beings. He makes scary gestures just to keep things under his control.

Meaning

The Devil shows the devilish side in us, the dark side in us that comes out unexpectedly at any time. It shows the needs, desires, and lust that are usually the ones which we need to bring under moderation.

It can show too much attachment to the materialistic world and its pleasures. The devil may have controlled you fully where you now feel captivated and find no way out. You may also be getting into too many sensual pleasures, that at time you feel as if you are just a puppet to some outer creature and have no control over your senses. Addiction to some materials along with addiction to sexual pleasures is signified here.

The Devil card coming up in a reading means that you are fully under control of your devilish side and feel helpless. But remember the devil is only as big as you make him to be. It resides in each of us and can grow only if you feed it. The goat won't come to you if you stop feeding it. It might wander for few days around you expecting food from you. Once it gets sure it will never bother you.

The face and expression of the Devil show that he is quite scary and demands us to stay in his control. But remember he also has wings, if you shoo him he will fly away.

The devil card is the fructifying of the Lovers card; the Lovers are here too much indulged into sensual pleasures. The Fool might be totally getting carried away with his senses.

Reversed

The reverse of this card actually shows good signs to come depending on the other cards in the spread. First of all this card shows that you might have freed yourself from unwanted bondage; if you haven't done so then you should do it now.

The Devil on the contrary also means getting detached too much from the sensual world. There might be a spiritual way that you might be heading to due to which you are putting away the materialistic desires to a halt. But don't forget that attachment is a part of life, living on this planet won't be easy if you don't accept the physical world in a physical body.

The two beings that were tied may have set themselves free. It may mean that the lovers surpassed the lustful desires and are moving ahead. But it may also show the lack of sensual pleasures in a couple's life; which is unfortunately setting them apart.

Also it shows that you may be well balanced. You don't get much preyed upon by the devil through a trap disguised as sensual pleasures.

Tower

Ruled by- Mars

Keywords- Breakdown, unexpected chaos, losing faith

Appearance

The Tower card shows a huge tower that's struck by a bolt from the skies. It seems that there were two people who were hiding in it for shelter who are falling down.

The tower is the Fool's journey where the fool has to learn lessons of separation, losing his faith, and learning to get out of the comfort zone. The Fool that was imprisoned in the previous card by a known external force (which he felt) is now attacked by some unknown external force. This place that he was living in was considered as it is safest but yet it as broken down by some bolt that came down from external force.

The Card also shows the breaking of the tower which shows the breaking of all that is old and is not needed. It can be physical resources or on a deeper level it may mean the beliefs that we hold that no longer serve us.

Also the figures are seen taking shelter, it might be a time for them not to rest and move on but they didn't do it; so nature fired them out of their shelter.

Meaning

The tower when appears in a reading clearly means that you need to break something. Appearing immediately after the Devil it means that you have to free yourself from unwanted attachment. Here there are shown two figures falling apart, which might signify the breaking of a relationship. Of course this is the one that is no longer serving its purpose.

The tower also literally means the moving of a house or reconstructing. It may also show renovation of your existing house.

The tower signifies that the place where you might be feeling very much safe and secure is actually the one that's most insecure for you.

It also means that you need to change your beliefs. There are certain times when we start believing in something, and when we have learnt that lesson we no longer might be needed to keep the belief. There are many such beliefs existing in our minds which we need to free ourselves from that will help us to grow further. Keeping these beliefs will not allow you to grow or will restrict your evolution on some level.

The card also says that the ones who are tied up by their senses as depicted from the precious card if don't give up too much indulgence into sensual pleasures or attachment or greed then ultimately nature will play its part to detach them from those pleasures.

Reversed

The card when reversed means that the place or people you trust and feel secure are actually reliable. You can put your full trust unto them. It also shows a relationship saved from breaking. It may either be a relationship of lovers, friends, business deal or any other close relationship.

This may also suggest that any change that needs to come into your life would come without destruction and devastation. Your change or transition will be carried out easily. Also nature will play its part in giving the least amount of bother to you.

Also this may show that some of the beliefs that you might be having are still serving their purpose. You need to stick to them. They might be either beliefs, techniques, or ideas that you need to keep to yourself.

The card reversed also affirms to you that you will not be facing great changes. It depends on the reading you are doing. Relationship reading may show no breaks and even if break up is inevitable then it would be smooth. Taking this card literally may show not to shift places now. It may be moving of the house or office; it may show a temporary stop in it or ask you completely not to make the shift depending on the other cards of the spread.

THE STAR

Ruled by- Aquarius

Keywords- healing, hope, humility, dream fulfilment, letting go

Appearance

The Fool is now here to learn some good lessons after learning the bad ones, he is here to learn something in a soft way, and yet the lesson is huge. But the fool has attained this state where he would learn from this soft learning too.

The Star appears with seven stars in the background with one huge star in the centre, the card is for beginning a Spiritual journey; the stars corresponds to the seven Chakras in our body and the central huge star being the point of enlightenment which you have to reach. The stars are eight pointed where eight is the number associated to abundance, signifying the abundant energy flow through the chakras.

The bird on the tree is a watch-guard of your spiritual progress. If you fall slow or stop the bird will wake you up and remind you to again start the journey will the same passion.

The lady is shown pouring water from two containers, one into the water and other on land. This shows her humility towards her service to Mother Nature. She lets in what needs to go to the water and helps the water that wants to run on land. Her nudity signifies her clear mind in doing the self-less act. The fruits grown on little plants on the land show the fruits of self-less service and spiritual growth and fruition of higher powers.

Meaning

The Star is ruled by Aquarius, and all the water energy used and showed so much in this card obviously signifies healing. As water is related to emotions and Love-energy is the best of all emotions. The card turning up in a reading suggests healing of anything it may be health, prosperity issues, property disputes, or any legal issue which could be resolved now. Star gives healing for all, involved in a particular situation.

The card also signifies the beginning of your spiritual journey. You may be considering to getting into spirituality but might just be feeling “will do it at the right time”. This card shows the “right time” for your spirituality has come. See for the adjoining cards for getting direction for your spiritual progress if you aren’t clear.

Also the lady is shown pouring some water on land and some water into the pool, her expression is serene. She is accepting the flow of anything that wants to go into its own direction. Also she is helping the water to flow in the direction the water wants. It also shows self-less service towards mother earth.

This card also signifies that your spiritual practices are fructifying or your self-less service which you were giving till now are starting to bear fruit. Remember these are just the initial stages of your journey. The lady is not seeing the fruits and so you too have not to work or spiritualize to get fruits. The night background also shows working at night, it may literally mean you might have to work in shifts.

Reversed

Reversed star may show getting away from your spiritual side or disconnecting temporarily. It also means nature wants you to stop here and lets you want to progress a little more in your materialistic life; the right time for the next spiritual dive would be made known to you.

It may show delays in healing or may show a prolonged illness. The illness may be on physical, emotional or mental level. To the least, this may point out to upcoming stressful times. The watery energy card when reversed may show an emotional block or blocked healing or prana energy. You need to “let go” what doesn’t want to stay with you. Freedom is what everybody wants and so respect people or events in your life that no longer want to be a part of your life.

The card also signifies the blocking of the chakras or energy flowing through it. The understanding and helping of Mother Nature with your self-less service will help you to release these chakras blocks. This also may be directly showing your expectations, from all the work that you are doing. The results won’t be satisfying till you attach certain expectations to it. Once you release all desires from it gratifying results will follow.

This also may be showing the gatekeeper or the logger of your spiritual practices might be giving you wrong signs. Or there might just be too much of negative energy that will be blocking your spiritual paths. Just release all of the negativity by practicing selfless love.

The Moon

Ruled by- Pisces

Keywords-

Fear, hidden dangers, surprises, uncertainty of what lies ahead, subconscious mind, cool moon energy.

Appearance

The appearance of the Moon card shows a big moon with a face in it. There is moon energy pouring down. There are two dogs howling at the face appearing from the moon. The two pillars that were lying behind in the priestess, hierophant, and justice cards appear here again. Just to show a little difference the Spiritual pathway is shown now open where in all the former cards it was hidden. There is a long road shown between the pillars showing the infinitely long way to the spiritual world of progression.

There is shown a crab which is crawling from the river bank, which is not noticed by the dogs. This points out to the danger of the dogs of getting bit by the creature. Also the crab appearing out of the blue on the path beginning shows the abrupt start of Spiritual path in anybody's life who is certainly not expecting it.

The face seen in the moon also shows hidden dangers, or dangers or disguised people in a fair garb.

Meaning

The Moon is a card of mixed interpretations, the upright card usually meaning something that sounds difficult for us to accept. There maybe people in your life that are dual faced, they are good in front of you and might be cooking different stories behind your back.

The moon energy pouring down like droplets also signifies that you might be very sensitive to moon phases, and note the phase that disturbs you and always prepare when that phase comes. The moon is also associated to our Ida nadi that is the cooler channel which passes through the left side of our body and is connected to our subconscious mind. You need to be aware of your subconscious mind. Learn about it, and try to program it only with positive things. Remove any fear that you might be having by planting positive affirmations.

There is a pathway shown entering the spiritual world, this card shows you the door to the spiritual world full of uncertainties. There is always a lot to learn on the way and you keep growing at each step and your growth never stops. You keep progressing higher and higher. This card may show your fear of the length of the spiritual path. Remember it's about the journey and not the destination.

Your mind might be affected with some disorder, you might be seeing different to what the actual reality is. The Fool is facing here his biggest fears in life. The fears are blocking our progress in life, which the fool is now confronting and has to discard them before moving ahead on the spiritual path. The spiritual path is full of uncertainties and fear always comes out of uncertainty or ignorance.

Note- Ida Nadi ruled by moon(left) and Pingala Nadi ruled by sun(on right) are energy channels that carry and distribute the warm and cool energies of the sun and moon inside our body; in order to maintain equilibrium inside us of these energy currents. To read more about this refer books on Yoga and Kundalini.

Reversed

The reversed moon actually is a positive sign; it means that you have already overcome your fears. There might have been things which were kept hidden from you which are now known to you. This knowledge might bring pain or sadness, but seeing the brighter side we can understand that the revelation was essential at this point in your life. People who might be acting sweet may not be really the same behind your back which now you have come to know.

The spiritual path might become easier for you as you start releasing all the fears and bitterness from your subconscious mind. Try improving yourself more and more as you keep releasing all that is unwanted. When you don't have the option to empty a bucket full of dirty water, it can be filled with clean water completely by continuously pouring clean water in it. It's the same with your subconscious mind you cannot empty it, but instead you can start filling it with positivity.

In a relationship reading this card turning up can show the 'changed face' of your partner, you might not be knowing their hidden moods/

faces which are now clearly seen. This may be painful to accept, see for the cards next to this card for the solution or result of it. If this reading is for any other relationship or family issue know that somebody's hidden conspiracies are exposed; look for who this person is by finding any court cards or other personality cards from the Major Arcana pack. If you don't find any, this may reveal some bitter feelings within your family.

In legal issues or property readings this would point out to exposing hidden factors that were working against you, the knowledge of this is tough but thanks to the reversed moon you may get the correct information.

The Sun

Ruled by- The Sun

Keywords- positivity, activity, rejoicing, life

Appearance

The appearance of the Sun shows us a huge Sun in the background with a face; sun is the giver of the life energy. The Fool is now getting the positive results of learning all tough lessons in the past. And now is bestowed with new life energy that is flowing into every cell of his being. He runs out with joy waving the flag he holds in his hands to express his happiness.

There are sunflowers shown in the background that signify that the sun has bestowed life energy for them too to bloom and be **alive.** The sun card shows a kid running on a horse, which is the fool who is now filled with energy and vitality like a child.

The kid is shown nude which shows freedom from all the baggage he had or the clarity of his mind. The horse on which he is traveling shows movement or time of action.

The fool's spiritual practices have brought him great rewards in his life.

Meaning

The meaning of the sun is first of all life; increase of life energy feels you coming back to life. You might be feeling gushing with some new energy and enthusiasm in your life for working hard. The card shows a horse, horses always signify action in your life. If there were stoppages or slow pace in your life or any other area of your life Sun promises them to catch pace with its emerging.

You may feel your life or yourself full of positive energy and happiness and vitality. Also this shows the selfless service of the sun towards our solar system. It keep glowing, setting and rising day by day; not for him but for the entire solar system, for all life on the earth, for you and for me. This card also might be pointing you to do selfless deeds to bring positivity into someone's life. The spread may also signify some specific person with cards ahead of it. Check any court cards or personality cards.

The sunflowers in the background show the positive environment around you, or it may suggest you to have fresh air and surroundings to help improve your vitality. The Sun is a tremendously positive card, because of the sun we all survive on this planet and so its presence in your reading brings lot of hope and improvement in health of the Querent.

This card does suggest the flow of positive energy, sometimes the Querent would say they are not feeling this way then the card had turned up as to alert the Querent to start thinking in a positive manner on a daily basis. Also the action or the work speeding up may not appear in the world then this card would suggest that the Querent starts speeding up their work, as he might be handling it lazily.

Reversed

The reversed sun shows a positive time that would be coming to a halt or it might show a stop in any progressive work. Either in a promotion, or a marriage or birth or signing that deal. Look for the surrounding cards to give the final verdict.

The actions might be suspended for no apparent reason; this card also shows laziness or depression. There would be lack of positive thinking in the Querent resulting in lack of positive environment. The person will be attracting people as negative, as he thinks.

The turning of this card in a health spread is not a good sign; it may show continuation of the ill phase. Also see other cards in the deck, the person might on a very negative mind-set that might be bringing him to such a stage, and he would need to become more positive minded to recover speedily.

Also literally taking the Sun in negative position would point out your weaknesses to accept the sun energy to its best. Remember to make yourself comfortable if you are in a too sunny area. Also if you are sensitive to the sun's energy try praying to the Sun to help you make only positive use of its energies.

The Spiritual path may not be giving you the positivity you expect so perhaps it might not the right time to turn to spirituality.

Judgment

Ruled by- Pluto

Keywords- release of unwanted, past life connections, rise high

Appearance

The Judgment card appears really as the Judgment Day or the time of renewal happening at the spiritual level. This is a very intense card for the Fool. The fool has to let go his blocks which he is carrying since his past lives.

The Angel with huge wings is seen blowing a trumpet as if alerting the souls that were lost somewhere to wake up and come back home. The spirits that were buried in their graves wake up and spread their arms as it saying they are ready for the change. It's a positive change for a spirit when it will get time to renew itself and choose another body rather than just being trapped in nothingness.

There are souls of all age groups found here.

Meaning

The judgment card shows a time in your life when years of hard work or suffering comes to an end. There might be some kind of long wait here it can be of anything that you were working hard on either a relationship, work, property or anything that now has the final 'hearing' as shown by the trumpet's blow. This can also point out towards any suffering which was prolonged either health-wise, relationship-wise, or any other area of life. But this card shows that the correct decision would happen. The Justice card was the 2nd phase of journey for the Fool where he learned that Justice will be done in the materialistic world; whereas this is on spiritual and Karmic level. "Anything never goes unseen from the law of Karma."

You might find good or bad happening, the bad might be in the sense that you know you have done bad and so would get a punishment. But you would be happy about it as these souls who were fed-up staying in nothingness are now ready to face their Karma.

The Angel above also expresses its presence all of a sudden; this assures that there is always a higher energy that would come to us at some time or the other in our life. If you are suffering and feel lost, then know this as a sign from the angels that they would be soon at your side to bring peace to you.

The ocean is also a sign for the subconscious mind, any big changes that occur might be from the materialistic level, or it might also be at the deeper subconscious level. Only when a person's subconscious mind lets go of something then he is said to be free from that issue or emotion. Otherwise till your subconscious mind is full of that energy you will never be able to be free from the feeling that arises as a result of that energy.

Reversed

The reversed judgment card shows delays in any right change that was going to happen, it will either postpone for time known or unknown depending upon how much of your Karmic debt is still left.

Any Karmic debt left in your account would make things difficult for you in any particular area of your life. You need to figure out why you are suffering from something; there always is a lesson to be learnt out of the suffering in our life. When we learn those lessons then we stop suffering and release the energy charge bringing in the pain. You need to find out what is this energy block that makes you suffer. An Energy block is brought in by negative feelings, and this might be any recurrent feeling that might be troubling you; anger, sadness, depression, greed, jealousy etc.

The card in reverse position may also point out towards a disbelief in a higher power due to prolonged suffering or waiting. When a soul has to pass through very difficult circumstances then they always wonder when the miracle would happen and often pray a lot for changes in their life. But when they do not see changes happening in their life they actually give up their faith in higher energy. This card may point out towards such a mind-set of your Querent or maybe somebody might be affecting his life due to it.

There is always hope at every stage of life, perhaps the appearance of this card shows that the phase of the Querent's life would end soon, but there's just a slight delay.

The World

Ruled by- Saturn

Keywords- Success, end of a phase happily, triumph, balance of all elements in your life.

Appearance

The appearance of the world card is a figure rejoicing its success, the figure is obviously the Fool who has learnt all lessons on the earthly plane and is now rejoicing. The cloth in which he tied a bundle of his Karmas is now wrapped around him showing that all the karmas and learning's are over, it's more on the spiritual level.

There are the four figures which appeared with wings in The Wheel of Fortune card are now without wings. Being with wings there was certainty and change in Wheel of Fortune but here the wings are gone and the mere creatures stay show grounding and solidity of this card. This is not the change of fortune bringing good or bad luck and bringing happiness that would soon change to sadness when the wheel turns.

[The wheel of fortune shows the unsteadiness of good and bad change in life by wings of creatures that surround it. But these very winds are now cut off and there is solid security and stability of the good that is achieved here. This usually is the highest good that the soul attains; the attainment of his life's purpose & ultimate purpose which is going to give him utter satisfaction. And this is going to last forever.]

But this is the card showing the phase of achievement and success for the soul which is everlasting. The learning of the soul always stays and the soul continues to evolve from the point where he stopped last. There is no downfall here, like gaining something in the materialistic world brings.

Meaning

The card shows success and ultimate feeling of fulfilment from your achievements. These achievements might not be as great as this world card shows, but they would be significant from the feeling they give to you. Your life would be going through ups and downs since long and the appearance of this card shows the inner level of satisfaction that comes from this card that has been reached.

There is also success into your life in materialistic world; this success might be on a very huge scale as we can figure it out literally from this card. There might be success that is noticed around the globe, also this might show a travel around the globe, or travel away from your country.

The leafy garland that appears around the rejoicing fool also shows achievement followed by some kind of scholarship or awards.

The fool has now become a success; he is recognized all over the world and so is no more a Fool. Any person who might be getting a progress report of himself in any area and has this card as the final outcome card, which would mean he has attained completion of that uneasy phase and succeeded in that area. When you learn from your sufferings you release all the suffering you feel this joy which is ultimate and everlasting.

For a relationship reading this may show a partner from across the seas.

Reversed

The reversed world card shows a delay in any kind of results that you were expecting for your hard work. It may also show delays in journeys or traveling or shifting a home. The shifting from home might be on a larger basis where you might be planning to move out of your state or country or even some place beyond the seas, it might be your dream place where you might want to live.

This card also shows delays in any good thing that you were expecting in any area of your life. This area can also be a relationship basis. It can show a delay in marriage or break of a relationship.

The World on a spiritual basis show that all lessons are mostly learnt only a little part is left. There maybe this little part left from the previous card of the Judgment. Look into yourself which part is not surrendering fully. Some part within you might not be ready to give up and accept just anything to bring a change. When you would do this your World card would be complete.

This card reversed also shows some kind of mourning or incompleteness. While positive shows celebration negative would show you the opposite of it.

The Minor Arcana

The minor arcana are comprised of four suits, the Wands, Cups, Swords and Pentacles. These all correspond to an element of our constitution and the 5th being our spirit itself. These all combine to form our body as well as the world and the universe around us. The soul usually selects several lessons to learn when in a physical body and the 5 elements support him in this mission. So the tattvas sometimes are seen working in our favour or sometimes against us.

The Swords are the suit of Air, air being the lightest is chosen as the first suit here as this suit would represent the least amount of **time**, to change. It takes just a second for our mind to change or decide something. And so I consider the swords having the least time duration. Swords with its quality of sharpness helps us to cut through illusion, confusion, stress, or any negative feeling of being stuck with a 'decision' for change and to grow.

The wands are the fiery suit, the next little more time consuming is the Fire. It takes a few minutes to strike a fire (of course when we try doing it the traditional way of rubbing two stones). So the next suit is the Wands, the fiery suit of Passions, Desires, Career, Work, Dreams, Enthusiasm, etc. The Wands are the fiery energy that follows the swords decision. Desire, Passion, Drive is always needed for fulfilment of any thought or decision.

The next suit that takes a little longer time then the above two is the Cups suit, cups are watery suit and as we know the cycle of water it takes fire to raise vapour and bring clouds and bring down rain. Raining is a longer procedure and it takes several months to gather enough vapour to form large clouds that would bring rain. The Cups are watery energy, what flows into you? Of course Emotions and feelings. And so this suit is for Emotions, Feelings, Love, Affection, etc. Emotions of Love bring fulfilment in life, along with decisions and actions and work.

The last suit is the earthy suit, the suit of the element earth, physical dimension; the one that gives you the physical body. This is the densest and so takes the longest time to change or create something. It's the suit of the materialistic world, resources, money, pleasures coming from luxuries etc.

Remember the above associations are my own, you might read some in a different way elsewhere. You can use anyone which you feel is comfortable to you or you can create your own, but whatever you create should gel with your gut feeling. Stay consistent with them.

The Minor Arcana

The Minor Arcana consists of 56 cards of rest of the Tarot Cards and which is further divided into four different suits which hold an elemental equivalent value.

Swords - The suit of Air. The least dense

Wands - The suit of Fire, a little denser then air.

Cups - The suit of Water, more dense then water.

Pentacles - The suit of Earth, the densest of all.

Starting with the Suit of Swords

The Swords suit is a mixed suit; it doesn't mean all positive when in upright position. Rather they turn out more when life is not going good, but their appearance of cards suggests action and decisions that will help make your life get good. The Swords are a suit of Mind, the mind is always wavering; your mind will be chaotic and disordered if you don't have any direction to take it into. When a soul isn't aware of its purpose then its mind is always wavering and chaotic. Once you know your purpose your mind gets direction where it has to focus. And then your energies can all be focused in that direction.

Swords deal with the mind, intellect, decisions, sharpness of persona, etc. Swords is a suit that will give you mixed meanings for upright and reversed cards. They are not always positive when upright and not negative when reversed.

Swords turn up at a time of difficulty when a "cutting edge" solution needs to be made to improve your life. Swords are blue coloured showing the cold colours of winters. The Swords is also a suit of mind and intellect. The mind has the power of taking decisions and thinking; which is the basic tool that helps us shape our lives, either in a good or in a bad way. A Swords person is thinking his way to make his life better whereas a Wands person is passionately acting his way to make life better, the Cups person is feeling or emoting his way to improve their life and a pentacle person materializes it out. This is how the entire cycle of manifestation gets complete.

The Ace of Swords

Appearance

The Ace of Swords appears with a hand holding out a Sword that's crowned, which shows the sharp and intelligent ideas coming out of the mind like a "crown" also the bluish hued mountains suggests the cold times in one's life that one has to change through the Sword-y decision.

Meaning

The Sword is a tool to help you get out of the cold situation in your life, your life would be hellish, or may seem to be steady and stagnant like the frozen snow which is why the sword suit is bluish in colour. Also the sword and the hands are shown glowing which says that the ideas or decisions that are flowing or you would take would need to be difficult and will help you to get out of the difficult situations.

The ace is a number of beginnings, new directions, or changes that are needed to be taken, remember here the decisions would be difficult; it's always with the swords as the suit that help to come out from difficult situations. When do people get badly stuck in their lives? When they let go off things easily to people what ought to be theirs. The swords are here to help these people be firm and decide the change in their lives.

Or this may be showing you a way to bring more joy into your life when you already are happy but want something more. The cards in the spread would show the level of goodness and the 'feel of it', what the Querent is feeling through right now. Whatever the current situation maybe, but the thoughts of the Querent show that they are lacking something and need to make their life more beautiful.

For a single person this maybe a thought of getting into a relationship, this person may be going through very cold feelings or may have gone through a failed relationship, this might be giving trouble to this person. He might be going through bad phase in life and just to change this phase he/she might be thinking to make a change in order to make life better.

It can also be a new idea to get out of a current mess the mess can be in any area of life, it can be a legal issue, a property dispute, downed career, etc.

Reverse

The reverse of this card shows indecisiveness in pinnacle decision time, you may lose good opportunities due to this. You can get to see cards next to it to get any cards that maybe pointing to help decide or bring clarity to the Querent's mind.

This card may show a dream not realistic that can be achieved but the ones that look like castles built in air, you cannot fulfil such decisions. The mind may be suffering from other blocks too which might be resulting into this.

A relationship reading with this card on important position may show that the partners might not be able to decide what they want in their relationship or what they want from the relationship. On a deeper level they might not be clear why they are into the relationship as none of them might be having feelings for each other. The relationship might be heading to fights and accusations. This card may also show the indecisiveness of one the partner for the relationship. The clarity that is missing would lead to unaffectionate behaviour.

Also this might be showing the delay of decisions in some serious matters, related to property or career or legal matters. The indecisiveness either the Querent or by someone else can be detected from any court cards and personality cards lying in important positions.

Two of Swords

Appearance

The appearance of two of swords shows a lady sitting on a shore with eyes blindfolded; she holds two swords in her crossed hands. The background is again cold and insensitive.

Meaning

The two of Swords shows a time in your life where you are confused between two decisions or thoughts in your life. These decisions may be equally weighing and important and now they would be creating confusion in your life as to which one you should select. Both the swords are appearing same in shape and size which shows you might be having equally 'sharp' decisions or thoughts which might be confusing you.

The blindfolded woman also signifies that you are not able to recognize the good or bad out of these two as your vision isn't clear or your thoughts are cloudy.

The situation in the Querent's life is cold and difficult; the lady is shown on a shore at night which is rare. People don't go to sea-shores at night. The night and darkness signified by the moon is showing the Querent's life is not in a good position. There may be a period of darkness as well as indecision so you need to make changes to improve it.

The sharpness of swords handled by somebody who is blindfolded is dangerous, signifying that the decisions or the ideas that are taken in hands of someone who is unaware of the gravity or seriousness of the decision to be taken. They may not deal well with the ideas or the ideas may hurt them in return if they are not handled well.

The swords appear too large for the person to handle; this may be the feeling of the Querent, as Nature assigns work to anyone which they are capable of. The Goals that you might have undertaken might appear dreamy and not realistic. You may not be clear of the goals and the way you will be completing them. The greatness or sharpness required would appear too large to you for these goals.

Also shows lack of Sharpness of mind and internal vision.

Reverse

The reverse card of the two of swords is actually a good sign, the card says that the indecisiveness or bluntness of mind that was there is gone now. There might be lot of clarity now in your life which will make it easy for you to make decisions that were pending till now. You may be very clear with which option you have to select.

The blur that you might have created for yourself in order to avoid the situation of taking responsibility is now intentionally removed by you which is a good move. Your life would pick up some pace now. The card is a good sign for showing the 'steady and stuck phase removal'.

It may also indicate a dark and confusing phase that might have just been stopped from coming into your life.

The Relationship spread will show more clarity which one to choose, the idea might be a little tough to implement but still you will be firm in your decision and the result of it would be a good.

Three of Swords

Appearance

The appearance of this card is with three swords piercing a heart. There are clouds with heavy rain in the background which also looks stormy.

Meaning

Sharp intellect cutting the heart, either of people you are concerned about in the reading or your own as your mind may be overpowering your heart's desires and are feeling discontent with the decisions that you take this way. This card may appear even if you are about to take such a decision this way, you may suffer long-term dissatisfaction out of this kind of decision making.

You may find people around that are breaking your heart, your desires are always kept unfulfilled, and this feeling will leave you shattered. You may be giving too much and getting too less than in return. When you feel this happening in your life there lie deeper problems with your self-acceptance or self-doubt in decisions you make. When you don't accept yourself in a certain way, then you will find people around you who will treat you this way. There may be some past mistakes in taking decisions that are now making you doubt your intelligence.

In life you will continuously face problems surrounding you that reflect problems that lie within you. You doing something wrong with you will slowly start showing up in your background and when you don't nip the problem in the bud it will escalate and then you will find people treating you very harshly and thus cutting you away from your heart's desire.

We do this kind of behaviour with ourselves because we don't know how to accept us when we make mistakes; we usually treat us stone heartedly as we are taught since childhood to feel guilty or to be not too self-centred. But in life, we are the most important person and attention and care needs to be given to ourselves too. We make mistakes but also need to be forgiven.

The more you have pierced your heart; you will find people doing it to you at the same degree. Furthermore if we take this card literally, it also points out "heart surgery" or any kind of physical damage/treatment to the heart.

Reversed

The Reverse of this card is a bit lighter and gives a relieving message to the Querent. The Querent might have moved away from a situation where he had doubted his own will.

You have brought an end to difficult relationships that kept hurting you, the decision indeed was difficult to take and put into practice; you did it and now will be rewarded with better relations. Life changes when you decided to make your life better by cutting away the unwanted relationships that clutter your mind.

When you move away from unwanted relationships, the void created by them is replaced by relationships that you now need to grow positively further, as it is your decision to live a better life by avoiding troublesome relationships.

This card also shows the healing of the heart physically and emotionally from a tough time. This card may also show that such a situation was dreaded but luckily it was avoided by you. The actual meaning also depends on the spread and cards surrounding this card.

The heartache is recently relieved or a sense of moving ahead from the heartache is felt by you.

Four of Swords

Keywords- Restlessness, fear, insecurity

Appearance

The appearance of the four of swords is shown with a man lying with his armour and swords all around him; three are hanging and one lying beside him. There is just yellowish colour on and around him whereas there is colour shown near his window.

Meaning

The four of swords means that you are overly concerned about your situation. Your situation might be just an ordinary one or one that doesn't need much attention; still you are giving all your energy and time to it considering it to be something big. Your worry is making the situation big.

You are too much insecure about your safety; your mind is getting overactive. The man is seen wearing an armour which already shows that he is secure; yet he has swords placed by his side to help him if needed, and with all this security too he is shown praying. We can also say it this way which is the best way; he only needs to ask for protection from a higher self rather than wearing such uncomfortable clothing and being so freaked out. Or he needs to just have faith in the Divine which will remove all these fears.

The colour in the room is mild and two toned, which reflects the cold feeling when one is insecure. There is just a stained glass in the room which shows that the outer world is colourful; only you have made your world colourless by building too much safety measures around yourself and having fear. Your fears aren't allowing you to see and feel the colours and happiness that lies already around you. Fears and negative feelings cloud our senses bringing only gloomy scenes to our mind whereas we can think positive from that moment itself.

This card also points out the fact that if you are too much insecure and you should connect to your higher self rather than taking any others help. Praying is always a better option and helps bring peace to the mind.

In a relationship reading this may show too much of protection towards oneself or possessiveness towards the partner. Your relationship might be missing out the beautiful colours in life just because of this.

Also this card shows the man in a praying position which looks much like meditation; the message is to build the inner strength needed by you with meditation; which is signified by the armour and prayer position. The card may literally mean to build safety for your-self, in the area of spread concerned.

Reversed

The reversed of the four of swords show that a time where you had to keep self-security is gone or changed. You might have developed some patterns for keeping yourself secure which are no longer needed. Life needs us to grasp and release certain patterns as it comes.

This card may also point out to the dangers of not protecting oneself. There may be dangers which might be in any area depending in what spread this card turns up; and you might not have sensed it. You need to keep certain safety measures.

The card also means carelessness towards one's life, there may be lot of matters which might be needing deep and serious thinking, which might be needing a bit of 'worry' but your attitude would be too neglectful of it.

This card says that resting time is over and you need to get up and get going for your work. It may also mean that you feel that you need rest and security, but this may just be your doubt, you won't need any rest or security. You may already be safe.

Five of Swords

Keywords- Fight, always winning attitude, put down people, never accept your defeat.

Appearance

The card shows that a man is standing with swords in his hands and few lie at his feet, also below his feet; he shows a grin which comes after winning in a war. There are two people shown in the background which makes us feel they are defeated by him.

Meaning

The five of swords first of all means that there is victory in a situation, an argument or a war where you proved your intellect to be true. You defeated others in the argument, this card may show an upcoming situation where you are concerned and the result would be in your favour. The card shows a man already winning by fighting which means that you have to fight the war in order to win it.

You may have developed an attitude where you always want to fight and win over a situation. The people around you might be getting hurt because of this attitude. You can lose sometimes in order to win somebody's heart. Showing your intelligence isn't always great. This card may also point out that you may have problems in your life because of you always wanting to appear superior and win over people in any situation. You may humiliate them just to make you appear smarter.

This card also promises you that you will win over a situation and so you have to keep your grounds and stay rooted to your truth. You will be supported only if you stand firm on our ground. Your past situations might have been unjust but the appearance of this card affirms that you will get a chance to defeat your enemies and prove your point.

On the contrary this card also shows that you might get defeated by somebody who just wants to prove themselves right. You may be depressed because of such a 'let-down' by them but this is not your let down, they are putting down the relationship just by satisfying their egos, in a relationship reading this card shows a red light to immediately take action if you are always made to feel 'defeated' or either this could be you who always wants to take the charge or dominate by proving yourself right. This will just make your partner fret.

Reversed

The reversed of this card shows that a time where you might have a conflict that has passed away or has been avoided, which is good.

This card may also show that you don't take your side when people try to fight with you or dominate you. You need to stand up for yourself. Your life might be having problems due to this. You will continue to have problems till you sort out this behaviour. Every person has to take care of their own selves and when you don't do it nature punishes you by sending difficult people around you who will continue to torture you until you discard this behaviour.

There are also chances that the people you have defeated are not done with you yet, they will again turn up to you and attack. You might think that they are gone and already have started to celebrate the victory.

Take your side when people are trying to defeat you for the wrong reasons, stand firm to your ground especially when you feel you are right.

If you are not getting the joy of winning then you are not in the right competition. Do what your heart pleases to do.

Six of Swords

Keywords- Travelling, safe journey, bright future across the seas.

Appearance

The six of Swords appears with a woman and a child sitting on a boat and a man probably looking like a Hermit rowing it. There are six swords planted on the boat, looking as if they are there for safeguarding the woman and her child.

Meaning

The Six of Swords means travelling, you will be travelling in distant lands. This will probably be travel with your family and not alone. The shift would be safe as there are swords kept with the woman and her child in the boat.

The waters in the distance look still and there are trees and lands on the other side, which means that the times after the shift will be pleasant and fruitful. The man with the oar rowing the boat is the one driving the direction of lives of the people which signifies that you should trust in the doings of the higher self. Let your higher self select for you the right path when you are not clear which way to go. The woman here is the wise one but she too is shown with her head lowered as if she doesn't have any hope or direction for the future.

The Swords planted in front of the people shows that they both are protected from the uncertainties coming to them. They don't need to fear for it, the same way when in life you don't know the direction then trust the higher spirit as you will be protected by the invisible forces of the sharp sword.

The swords being taken all the way overseas also show that you need to carry your defences everywhere you go. Also this card shows that you just need to carry your defences and 'show them' you won't need to use them.

This card also warns to practice safety measures while travelling; it may just be your daily commuting to and fro from work.

Reversed

The reverse of this card shows that there may be delay in your travels or journey or there may be a delay in your journey that was decided to start right on.

The card also shows that you may not have your defences with you at right time; you may not be 'safe' on the move. Your journeys might not be safe or planned. Look for signs before moving any further. Also see for cards accompanying this card to know more specifically what this card means.

You are ought to move out from the place you are at present, the place is not for you which you already know but you don't want to leave. You may not want the change to adapt the new shift in your life. Life always needs to change when one phase is completed and another phase needs to begin, the physical world may need to have this shift or even the shift of thoughts. Thinking with a broader perspective will help you to change your current state of mind. You may not be done with the current situation that you need to leave and move on. Or maybe there may be something still needed to learn from this situation and so it's not leaving you.

Seven of Swords

Keywords - stealing of ideas, objects

Appearance

The seven of swords shows a man with a bundle of swords running away, and he looks around stealthily to make sure no one sees him. There are people sitting in a distance and the tents are empty due to which this man has made this move. He has stolen something, or taking away what was not his own.

Meaning

The seven of swords show that a man is running away with swords and the feel is that he might have stolen them from the tents that belonged to other people. There maybe people around you who might be stealing things from your surroundings or it may be ideas that might be stolen. The card says that things are stolen and you don't know about it. Or either things are about to get stolen without your knowledge and this card is giving you a warning.

On the contrary this card may also mean that you are stealing things from others what does not belong to you. You might also feel like stealing ideas of other people that are potentially more rewarding, and might give you a raise at work. Remember that karma strikes back; you don't need to do this. Keep away from the greed of having more if this card appears.

This card may also point towards the fact that there is a danger of keeping your things, objects, or ideas under others' supervision and they might get stolen; you might not be given your own things easily which this card says should be taken away stealthily.

The man also is not taking away all the swords, so this card might also point out to you to say take only what is needed and leave the rest for others. This card may also show that there are deceptive people around you who might steal under your nose and with a smiling face; without you even guessing it.

Also this card shows the man smiling with the swords he has in his hands, it's a sign that you should be happy with whatever you have and also be content with what other people are having.

This card also shows that things that are important to you, you have a fear of them being stolen from you and you need to be careful about it; as this might also be your gut feeling warning you of incoming danger.

This card also shows weak memory, or important thoughts slipping out of your mind that might raise worries.

Reversed

The reversed of this card shows that the things that were stolen are now retrieved back. The person that was doing this might be caught or may himself come forward and accept his sin.

This card also shows that if you have stolen things you should give them back, you can put them back secretly or by coming out in the open. The card also suggests that the greed that made you take away or steal things has gone and you now might be feeling guilty for stealing things against the wish of others.

This may also show that your things that were stolen don't hold any value or importance to you and so their being stolen doesn't matter to you.

This card also shows that people, who had gone away from you, might come back to you. This card also shows improvement of memory as the swords is the card of intellect.

In a relationship reading this might show the regaining of interest in a partner. It also shows the coming back of a partner.

Eight of Swords

Keywords - blinded vision, lack of clarity, confusion, tied-up feeling, and movements restricted.

Appearance

There is shown a lady, arms tied at her back, she is blindfolded, which makes her judgment difficult plus there are several swords around her that can prove dangerous if she moved.

Meaning

This card appearing shows a difficult situation in your life, you feel tied up or are really tied up to the rules and regulation or traditions that are not allowing you to do something which you feel you must be doing. Also at the same time your vision or sight is also not clear and you cannot see things and decide clearly; and on top of it the surroundings are such that is harmful if you take any wrong step as depicted from the swords planted around the lady. The entire plot points out that you are giving away your controls to others who are now tying you up. People cannot do this to you unless you permit them to do. The very first thing to move out of this situation is to trust on your instincts and take a move. This situation shows terrible troubles and confusion and lack of faith; but lack of faith can only be restored by starting to trust in yourself, the beginning might not be good but keep having undivided faith in yourself till things start getting well.

It shows there is utter confusion everywhere, inside as well as outside of you. In a relationship reading this might show indecisiveness of any of the two partners, or this might show the way in which the relationship is heading. In any other reading this might show the confusion of the Querent that is making them indecisive in this situation.

There is a way out of this situation right in front of the figure where there is no sword planted, or this is the direction to move; the card suggests that you are blindfolded and restricted of moving of your sides or going back so the only option left is to move ahead. The feelings may not be good also your mind is not clear but keep moving ahead.

Reversed

The card reversed shows that there is clarity coming into your life after great disorientation. There may be obstacles in your life yet you are very much sure and focused for what you want to do in your life.

This card also shows that bad times are gone, your confusion state has now turned to clarity, your ties are all loosened, your path is clear to move on. You feel freedom pouring in. Also this card signifies that you were tied up by your own narrow beliefs and thoughts which you have now freed yourself from and are enjoying life from a much higher perspective.

You were feeling that people were controlling you till now and felt tied up which is now eased. You no more feel tied up by the environment and are able to move freely; freedom of thoughts, freedom of movement, freedom of seeing things with a clear perspective.

Nine of Swords

Keywords- crying, great sorrow, guilt, misery, difficult or dark times, dark night of the soul.

Appearance

The appearance of this card is simple and signifies the meaning directly to us. The figure in the scene is shown on the bed not sleeping but crying. It seems that she is having a difficult time, and is crying alone in despair. There are swords on the wall. The blanket the figure is covered with shows the pictures of all the sun-sign symbols and there are roses alternating between them. The darkness depicts night time, or the dark time during one's life.

Meaning

The card says that you are having the darkest time of your life, you have lot of sorrow that is making you awake at night plus you don't have anyone to share your tears or sorrows with. Difficulties seem to have clouded your vision and you are left with no choices except to do with what you have or that too would have been taken away from you. Life seems to have taking your worst of tests and you feel bitter as you don't know what to do in this situation.

There are tough times in one's life only when we are not doing what we ought to do. When we are on our life's mission's path we have everything we need to make ourselves comfortable at all levels physical, mental and emotional levels. But when we move away from our life's path then resources start depleting, and also mental and emotional balance started disrupting. Life gives us signals at all times, for what to do further. When we are doing the right thing it gives us good signals and when we are doing badly it makes our life difficult. Find out what is it that you are doing that is not right for you to do in your life.

There are always light hints moving in our minds that make us feel that we are not doing the right things. Find out this and start working by making this wrong thing right.

The astro-signs covered on the bed sheet also show that planetary positions are at their worst bringing the worst in your life. And the toughest of times is now going on or is to come in near future. But the roses aligned alternately with the astrological signs say that though there are tough times yet there are still roses beautifying your life. Or this also says that the best of roses (learning to evolve) are going to get bloomed during this time.

The card also may literally mean insomnia.

Reversed

The card reversed shows that there were tough times that you have seen but now they have moved away and a bright morning has begun on the horizon. Your life's difficulties have ended or have begun to lessen now.

The planetary positions that were working against you are now begun to change and the planets have started to work in your favour. The right clarification of the planets that might be signified here would be on the cards surrounding this card, also see the positions where these card lies.

The card depicts one of the toughest times in life of a man, the dark night of the soul which is extremely difficult to deal and brings immense pain and suffering but the reverse says that these times have receded and good times have started or the dark night have gone and new dawn has begun to arise.

Ten of Swords

Keywords- back stabbing, betrayal, health crisis, resting period

Appearance

The card appears as if its night time, a man is lying stabbed in his back in a lonely place, means he wouldn't be looked after here. The night time can also be taken as the dark times in one's life where one feels no way out of the darkness, this man was betrayed, back stabbed and lies dead and defeated. There is light seen in the distance which says that the darkness would be replaced by light soon. So there is still hope.

Meaning

The ten of swords is one of the worst cards that can turn up in your reading; swords are usually the difficult times in your life. Here too the man is seen lying face down with 10 swords stabbed in his back, and one half of his body is covered with a red cloth. The feeling of grief, pain, defeat, failure, and betrayal of the worst kind comes with this card. You are going through a dark time in your life, where things seem beyond your control, your life too is out of your control, and there are things that are yours but are taken away from you. You couldn't even say 'no' for it. The darkest time in anybody's life is shown by this card.

This card also shows that you would be facing or will face shortly a time when a person you trust most will backstab you. You need to stay alert for this. While staying alert won't lessen the pain as the harm to be done to you has already begun, but staying alert will help you to save the remnants that you still have with you.

This also shows literally some problems with the back and some surgery related to it, if not the back then your body might be very much weak and you need to take complete rest in order to recover fully.

The ten of swords is a swords suit so it's possible that there may not be the physical hurt involved represented with this card but there may be this feeling of betrayal and backstabbing in your mind.

This can also show that you might be behaving this way for someone, the card turning up in your spread only states that your karma will fire back and what you have done will soon come to haunt you in your life. So if you are planning to do this to anyone think twice, and proceed.

This time may seem the dark times that would never end, the message of this card is just soothing in this case as we can see light in the background of this man; the message is "there is light at the end of every dark tunnel" plus the message is more promising the darker the time held longer the duration will be exchanged for an immensely bright and positive future.

This card also warns you to stay alert and not allow any parasites to breed around you.

Reversed

The reversed of this card is actually a good sign, there was deep sorrow, despair, betrayal, in your life which has now been shaken. You have recovered from the pain of this shock and have begun to live a better life. Your sorrow, grief, and feelings of being hurt by others have healed, and you have learnt a lesson from it and are now moving on.

This card also shows that the negativity that comes with this card has been dispelled and you were easily saved from the wrath of this card.

Recovering from an illness, improvement of health, positivity entering into your life, and a new start after a breakdown.

Reversed this card also shows that there was a situation like this which might have hurt you but it would never happen. Your alertness is helping you not to get into such ruts.

This also might mean that you are stepping into the light after spending time in darkness. You are getting out of the grief after depression; you are trying to live your life once more after facing a life-threatening situation.

Page of Swords

Keywords - Restless, hyperactive

Personality

This can be a young child male/female slim body (as they are very active), they will show these qualities very often. Also adults and elderly people can show off these qualities.

Appearance

The page appears here with a sword in his hands, the surroundings around him show land with distant mountains, the trees as well as the hair of the page show that there is a high breeze blowing. The clouds appear moving at great speed too. There are birds seen above the clouds, the main idea of this card seems 'air' energy at its high.

Meaning

The page is a young lad in his/her childhood days; his mind is hyper alert and changes at the flip of a hat. The surrounding of the page is also seen airy, which means there is an environment around this kid which is making his mind this way.

The page of swords is also about the beginning of any new ventures, especially with great pace and enthusiasm as the breezy energy of this card reveals. The pages are here for giving an idea about starting a new project, the continuation of an old one whether done or not; depends upon the other cards in the spread. Pages are also projects in their infancy; just an idea popping up to make a better future or present is denoted by the pages. The pages require the energy of the knights to keep continuing the project in order to get the full advantage of the idea.

The page is also a fugitive type of person who cannot stay at one place, with the quality like the air which always keeps blowing. The page of swords is also a person with a shaky mind; they change their decisions at the flip of a hat. They can be very serious at a time and at the very next moment burst out laughing. Their might lose their temper in an instant but they cool down very quickly.

The page is about intelligence, decisions, and the power of one's mind, communication, and reflection of thoughts. The page is calm but doesn't look so; the page is quiet but doesn't seem so as they might give out a sermon whenever they feel necessary.

Reversed

The reverse of the page of swords too much air energy that is suppressed and not allowed to flow freely, such a person may become irritable mentally and physically. Their physical body will always keep suffering from minor ailments due to the blockage of air energy or thoughts in the mind.

The page reversed also shows an individual who is very confused and always dreamy as to how to use his energies or use his decisive powers. He may appear always in a dreamy state or his conversations might be too difficult to understand. His ideas can be blunt or vague without appropriate edge.

The restricted flow of air energy in your life, this means lack of new ideas, memory weaknesses, low recall ability etc.

Your mind may be wandering to places it likes yet you are forcibly diverting to thoughts that seem logically ok. You cannot think or be this way, the mind always drifts to the things it likes and would go just that way.

Knight of Swords

Keywords- pace, hasty, high temper, quick actions, hates slowing

Personality

This can be an adult person male/female lean bodied, with the qualities listed. It can also be a very young person trying to behave as such or a very elderly person who shows these qualities.

Appearance

The knight appears as speeding into the scene on his horse; horses show action in every card they appear. The land around him seems like the barren land of any desert, the trees also appear as if blown by strong winds. The horse looks as if the knight is making him speed too much. There are birds drawn on his cloak and the horses rein signifies air energy. The knight's armour has a wing-like shape at his knee which means that the knight although has enough speed yet wants to speed even more.

Meaning

The meaning of this card is clear; it signifies a person who is too hasty in his actions. It can be either male or female doesn't matter. They always have a habit of finishing their tasks early before time. They cannot go slow at any cost. If they ever have to slow down they would get bored. Getting slow is never their MO, if they do then there is something wrong with them. They are always naturally hasty.

This pushes them into making quick decisions and putting them quickly into action, the problem here arises is that they tend to get bored soon and cannot fulfil their work taken at hand. They tend to leave their tasks undone half way. They are very much interested in planting the trees but don't have the patience for the saplings to grow.

They have this hasty nature which might also be bugging people around them, they would themselves take in a lot of work and push on more to others as well which might be tiring them. They usually have this habit of coming and going in a snap and so usually don't notice the people or things that were around them. This might make people feel neglected, keep things scattered.

These kinds of people are very impatient and cannot do tasks that require slow and steady work and attention. They don't like doing small regular tasks like arranging their wardrobe or office table as these according to them isn't much productive work but like this work to be done for them.

Reversed

The reversed of this card means lack of pace or speedy action at peak times when speedy actions are needed. There may be lack of enthusiasm in the project or you may feel out of mood, it maybe some work that doesn't please you at all and so you cannot stand it just for the sake of just doing it.

You may be lacking the enthusiasm while your surroundings may also be lacking the pace and speed that pleases you. Life may seem locked in a phase and not moving ahead or events seem to take place too slow while you might get frustrated looking at the pace other's life is going with.

Problems with putting plans into action, deciding and taking action upon it may seem at a miles length. There will also be a lack in one's own desire of working with speed. You may feel quite depressed, as if your life's enthusiasm is sucked away and never going to return.

This may also show the worst in the environment, the desert that was blowing in the upright position might be now untamed with the reverse position. You may feel things getting out of hand in your surroundings.

Queen of Swords

Keywords-Dominance, power, sharp mind, decisive, strong willed, Independent

Personality

This lady can be a middle-aged female with the qualities given above, fuller body; also it can be a very young person male/female who might be displaying such qualities and maturity.

Appearance

The queen appears facing her side with a sword raised as if demanding explanations from someone. She looks strict and stern, wants her work done and then uses her feminine nurturing nature. She cannot be hard on you if you haven't fulfilled her orders. There are huge clouds in the background that show a liability of a storm; very likely. You can face a storm if you don't fulfil her orders. There is a stream of water in distance which shows her rare emotional nature.

Meaning

This card shows a person of somewhat mature age who holds a reputed position in some organization or a household. She is very strict and cannot take dishonesty. Her rules are very rigid and written on a stone, and she doesn't like rules to be broken or commands disobeyed. She handles all her matters by herself and sees each and every work that is done to utter details. Queen of Sword females are usually highly analytic and rational in their behaviour rather than loving and sensitive. They can be nerdy, with sharp minds and memory. They have a very powerful memory for remembering things she wants to remember.

She is also very good at judging, judging just about everything she can try on, judging the behaviour, work quality, people etc. Her ability makes her quite scary for people working below her.

This card may also show a male with these qualities, a man who can be hard, strict and stern at the time when work demands. Else they are quite caring and sensitive.

Freedom and independence at their peak make the best use of this freedom. You may be having a lot of responsibilities, but you need to put 100% focus at one job at a time when needed. Distribute your energies equally to all tasks you handle.

Reversed

The over use of analytical skills just over everything, you try honing your skills at every area possible. This may thin out your ability as you become shallow whence your area isn't concerned. Try developing your skills in just a particular direction, this direction can be peculiar to your talents and abilities.

You may be acting too soft towards others who need to be dealt with caution and strictness. You might be underestimating yourself. There might be lack of confidence in one's judgmental powers or analytical powers.

It can also be a young/old male trying to be too feminine and not taking his life seriously.

There may be wandering of self elsewhere from the actual work that needs attention. Too lenient. The required degree of strong mindedness isn't present.

King of Swords

Keywords- Agile, sharp minded, sharp tongued, in-conquerable mental abilities, verbally unconquerable

Personality- This is a male/female, tall and lean bodied, appear quite restless from their structure, this can also show young adults with these qualities but with the perfection of the air suit.

Appearance

This king looks slim and tall, sits on a throne with a bare sword. There are still trees in the background unlike other three court cards of this suit. The clouds also appear still and receded. The birds seem to fly peacefully in the sky.

The king is on a throne that has butterflies carved on his throne, which signifies the light nature of this king.

Meaning

This person will be very strong willed but very light hearted and jolly. They will take it as if life is very easy for them, but from within they possess the unbendable focus that only the master of this suit can possess.

He looks easy to handle but still possess the qualities of 'steadfastness' and 'not accepting failure at any costs' attitude. He can be pleased by doing his work with perfection and honesty. His mind is very sharp and focused, cannot get disturbed by anything. They can be in the middle of a crisis and yet be very much calm and focused on his work.

Their work of action is what counts everywhere, it can be in any field but needs that piece of work to be acted upon and finished with perfection, sincerity, honesty and timeliness. He never compromises with the qualities above. They need to be put all into a job to be done.

The sword he holds is usually just on show for intimidating people, he is soft hearted and would never act harsh but will never forget to use the sword to threaten, for those who don't work well, according to his commands.

It can also be a young or middle-aged female with these qualities.

Act well without getting threatened but remember a sword still exists if you aren't honest. Life will be easy right now but yet don't forget to fulfil your duties at the right time.

Reversed

Lack of trust in one's abilities or lack of persistence, in any kind of work at hand. Impatience, frustration, lack of tolerance, cannot wait when time slows to a halt. This person would be difficult to handle and understand as he doesn't know himself what he wants and how much he wants which makes him this way.

This man can also be rash and violent if his ends are not met. He uses his powers to threaten and dominate people. He gives huge promises but cannot fulfil them. Also he is used to curse when 'his' way or order isn't followed. He is quite disoriented with his own thoughts and promises and so he often panics and runs away at the time of need.

This kind of man cannot be trusted when given responsibilities and handling money or other important and valuable objects. Stealing, treachery, fooling is common to his nature, and he can cross any limits to make his ends meet.

This can also be a female, young or middle aged, with these qualities. If young see for the ability of an expert in her doing of acts.

Suit of Wands

The wands is a suit of fire element, a warm suit that carries fiery energy with it. Fiery energy is needed in our life at every moment. For any thought we think, to put into action we need the fiery energy of passion, ambition, dream building, aiming, courage, confidence, talents, and the abilities to fulfil them.

The creative fire in us when balanced works out well and usually doesn't need any attention. This creative fire knows where to flow and usually makes people comfortable doing things this fire can create. This fire goes out of balance when there is an obstruction in its flow. Creative energy when flows freely, creates something good or else its starts self-destructing from where it is to be released so that it can move places to get a fresh start and do things it needs to manifest.

Wands is a suit that usually signifies our career, talents, work and direction to take our life unto. They also stand for your life purpose and life's mission.

Fire is second to the air suit as fire would burn more brightly when air blows stronger. Passion would get stronger when you keep feeding it with appropriate thoughts.

Ace of Wands

Keywords - Beginning a project, initiating work, new step further

Appearance

The ace of Wands appears like all other aces with a hand appearing from a cloud and offering a wand. The wand is creative energy and the hand appearing out of nowhere means new opportunity for work, career, or any creative project would come out of nowhere like a helping hand offered by God at the time of need.

Meaning

This card means you would be getting new projects, ventures, creative ideas to work upon and soon you may already have started working on it. You might be having a project idea in your mind or anything creative to put into action, this card shows a green signal and commands action to be put on it.

Ace of wands brings the promise of growth with every idea you put into action. The thing is you need to put it into action right now as this card has appeared. If you have 3-4 different ideas then go with the idea that is best according to you and you feel prepared to start up.

The wand that appears has fresh leaves growing from it, this itself gives a promise of growth with any plan that you put into practice. There is a building like a castle seen in the background as well as a stream of water; this signifies you should use this creative force to build your dream castle. It can either be a castle or something which you always dream of.

This can also be an opportunity that is brought in by someone that will help you fulfil your dreams, this can be anyone your friend or family or maybe from a stranger; but the news would ring up a bell in your heart. You would know this is the right opportunity for yourself.

Reverse

The reverse of this card can show that there are many options or opportunities in front of you which is making you confused where to go and what to choose. This also arises when your mind isn't focused or sure for what it wants to do. A period of wandering around opportunities, there may be potential opportunities that can bring you good returns in future. This also maybe a time to know what you really want to do in your life, and confusing opportunities are only helping you to bring clarity to your mind. The difference can be made clear with cards accompanying this card in the reading, see future card after this card.

The card reversed may also show lack of enthusiasm or creative force to initiate something. You might be having a bunch of ideas and projects but lack the will to put them into action. Laziness or shunning of responsibilities may also be the reason for this.

This also shows that it's not the right time to put your plans into action; you may still have to plan out more or wait for a better opportunity.

This card can also show the presence of opportunities (like presence of all resources for starting something new) but the idea may be missing or the passion might be gone.

Two of Wands

Keywords - Give out, globalize, open doors

Appearance

This card appears with a man standing between two wands and is offering a globe, his expression is confident. He is offering something from the world to the world outside him. The environment around him is pleasing and calm as if of a town or a city. There is water seen in the distance.

There are flowers embedded into the wall where he is standing. One wand is in his hand and the other is suspended from a wall next to him.

Meaning

There is something creative you can give. This can be the area around you, your workplace or city or the world. You have a creative idea, talent, gift, or any other ability with which you are quite the expert and can offer it to the outside world. Your passion, zeal, willpower etc. might be needed somewhere outside the area where you currently live. Step out and let your creativity take you to greater heights for success.

An overseas journey regarding work or projects might be headed soon, or you need to plan out for such a journey. You set the plan and nature will help you manifest it with the energy of this card. This card also might show you that someone across the seas might be interested in your creativity and offer you a job to work with them or for them.

This card also shows growth of new ideas as an on-going process, the idea at hand and its growth would be immense. It has promise for growth, not singly but doubly (as two wands are sprouting).

The building also looks like a fort which means that you might get an opportunity to work in a better organization or one which might lead to connecting your work abroad.

Reverse

The reverse of this card means blockage of any opportunity that was coming your way for broadening your work prospects. This may also be the delay of the opportunity, or loss of a potential opportunity that was going to prove beneficial for you.

This also shows a lack of enthusiasm to step out of your comfort and go out into the world for succeeding and growing. This might also be due to the lack of creative ideas.

There might be obstacles in the way of you getting out and working in order to succeed, perhaps you make your life difficult by letting people interfere into your career or professional life, which is now becoming a big problem. People are not allowing you to grow freely, "a frog in the well" feeling.

Restricted thinking due to lack of contact with the outside world. Grounding missing, you don't like to reach out to the outside world due to too much self-indulgence. You lack grounding, and feel the world is not a place for you to live in.

Feeling of hatred for the world as you aren't able to make a mark in the society, and as a result you stay cut off from the society.

THREE OF WANDS

Keywords- waiting, wait for the world to respond, anticipation

Appearance

There is a man seen standing in between wands as if he is waiting for something or someone, there are boats or ships that are seen sailing in the distance. This man looks as if he is waiting for these boats to come ashore.

Also this man may be a merchant who is waiting for his goods to arrive, after paying the money or waiting for the money after doing the work.

Meaning

The card shows waiting period after you sow the seeds of your creativity. Any work done doesn't pay off immediately; here you need to wait for the results to appear. You might have to wait for the money that might come in as a result for the world you put in. Or you might be waiting for the result of your work after putting in your creativity.

You will have to wait, wait for the results. The accompanying cards may show you whether you need to keep purely waiting or start doing some other work in order to kill the anticipation.

The wands planted also look like saplings that are waiting to grow into trees; you have put in your effort and now have to wait for the project to grow.

Hold onto your ideas as you allow them to grow, progress will happen in the same direction you are planning to go, and already have started working upon.

If you have been thinking twice for the current work you are putting efforts into due to people questioning you; then stand firm on your grounds. There is 'wait' written here, but there is also sure success in your hands in future.

Till you don't receive proper successor growth, don't squander much on unproductive resources.

Reverse

Restlessness or impatience is seen, due to prolonged waiting period. You might feel as if you are waiting forever and not going to get any results. You feel like giving up at midway.

Negative mind set not letting you to think good and persist on your plans. You keep quitting your plans as you are too impatient.

Reversed, this card also says you don't need to keep waiting for this thing to show results. Instead start working on some other creative project.

This card may also point out that you won't be getting any results from this work, so you need to stop waiting for the results and move on. You need to come up with something that would be needed at the workplace or needed by people.

There may be delay in getting results or the presents that you are expecting. They might also get lost in the way. The ship you are waiting for might not come ashore or might get delayed.

Four of Wands

Keywords - Family, marriage, celebration, rejoicing, reunion

Appearance

This card appears with two figures rejoicing in the background, there are four wands arranged and flowers on top of them as an adornment. There are people seen in the background talking in a get together, the castle is decorated for this celebration.

Meaning

Marriage is on the cards, you will be getting married soon. Also this card may suggest that the person you are with is the right person to get married to. This may also show a marriage in your family or some near relatives or close friends. This card can also show a celebration at workplace, probably a promotion or a farewell to someone.

There can also be a get together in your workplace or study which would be a remarkable event. A time for celebration and growth in your life, marriage time; the time to turn into two from one. And similarly this card can signify growth in any area the reading is done for.

Satisfaction, contentment, happiness are all predicted by this card. These feeling are to prevail into your life, or the changes might have already started happening by now. A card for settlement, settling into new house, or renovation of an existing house. Also inauguration of new house can be depicted, as this is also showing a celebration and house is shown in the background.

Turning back home after a long journey of months or years, or getting back home after a great dispute or fight. Or you might feel like reconnecting to somebody from your home whom you had broken contact with; reunions.

Reverse

There would be a delay in marriage, or the marriage that was scheduled would not take place at all. Also it shows problems in the current marriage, it also shows divorce or break of marriage. If you are not married then this card turns up then you would have problems with your partner.

A celebration very badly conducted or cancelled causing pain to you, a delay in celebration, problems in your family, and causing the family to break and move apart. Somebody outside of your home might be causing problems for your family.

Feeling of insecurity, loneliness at home. The family that exists doesn't seem to exist at all from emotional level. Feeling aloof from all your loved ones, relationships are a place where we can come to, to feel loved and cared. But this card may show that even though you may have these relationships they lack this charm.

Being thrown out of the house, homelessness, or being devoid of job or workplace. Your existing workplace might be taken away from you leaving you without shelter. Legal matters for property can consider this reverse card as a defeat of the matter.

This could also show a celebrative moment turning into a pain-giving one.

Five of Wands

Keywords- Fight, clash in views, controversy, conflict

Appearance

This card appears with five people holding a wand each, and fighting with them. Everybody seems to be using their own might to their fullest yet no one seems to be winning. The fight looks like never ending as no one is giving up and everyone seems to show they are not less than the others.

Meaning

You might be in a situation where you are fighting with others involved in it, or trying to prove your point endlessly. There are other people too here but they too want to prove their point. Everybody wants to prove their point and nobody wants to listen. You should act wisely.

This card also shows there is only enough space where the fight is occurring, means you have to pass through the situation rather than just backing out or walking away from this situation. This card also shows challenging situations where you will be faced by equally challenging opponents. If this is in your case then you need to prepare yourself well for this as all are equal powerful.

In such a situation where all are equally strong and the fight seems unending then the solution lies in your mind. A mind is more powerful than muscle power. Think of a powerful idea to help you out of this situation. Or this card may also show a situation where you would need more of your mind power along with muscle power to get out of it.

This conflict can also be an inner conflict where you might be fighting between different thoughts or beliefs, which to discard and which one to still keep.

This card also shows a struggle with people amongst the same family or under the same roof it can be your office, home or playgroup. It can be a playful fight or a real and serious fight. This card might also show that the fight or conflicts you are in are just a waste of time. They are not going to yield anything, so it's no use being in this situation anymore.

This can also show a game or a sport where people practice their skills on each other.

Reverse

This card when reversed shows that there is a situation where a fight can arise but it can be avoided or subsided. Or it can show that such a situation might have arisen but has naturally subsided.

This also shows that if you have a nature of keeping on fighting, then you need to put down that urge to stop fighting and let go sometimes. Don't try to prove yourself correct all the time. Some matters would be solved without fighting so try to handle all matters without raising a fight.

This card also might show an attitude where you never fight or try to take your side or prove your point. You might be into self-sabotaging behaviour. You need to take your side and stand up for yourself sometimes when it comes to your self-esteem or self-respect. Try to stay firm grounds when anyone challenges you this way.

This also shows that any situation that you feel would raise a conflict which actually won't need any fighting or controversy. Any result expected out of this situation would be achieved easily.

Six of Wands

Keywords - victory, applause, fame, praise

Appearance

The card shows a man seated on his horse holding a wand that is decorated with foliage. There are people around him holding a wand each; they all are in a procession like a celebration of a victory. The man is happy and also the people seem happy. The horse too shows a pleasing look towards the man who is riding it. The horse wears a green covering which looks a rich velvet type.

Meaning

This card means Victory in all your undertakings; you might be doing some work that would surely become as a success. If you want to know the success of any work/job that you wish to proceed with, then this card shows certain success.

You are about to get famous or recognition for your achievements or your good work. This work can be anything, your career or some community work that you might be doing for the welfare of people, or some work that would benefit a larger amount of people. Your work will prove beneficial to people or perhaps make their life easier. If you haven't achieved these results then this card says you should keep working on any projects that would be helpful to society.

Hard work, toil, extra work, and overtime all these would now fructify. You will bear the sweet results of all the work that you put in till now. Or you might have already started to get the results or greeting for it. It's time for you too to acknowledge your success. Thank yourself for putting in hard work.

Celebrate your success along with others celebrating for it, you have put enough energy to your tasks and a pat on your back is needed too.

Your work has succeeded to such an extent that you feel each and every being around you is congratulating for it. Express your gratitude to your creator for helping you do this much hard work. Also if you are working for some project then this card shows great success with it. Ask your creator to give you the strength and will to work for it.

Praise, happiness, cheering all happening for you; on your side.

Reverse

The reverse of this card shows you getting infamous, you might be at a good position where people might know you for your work and abilities but this card's appearance shows a dark spot on your conduct which people might consider. Your current work might not be as good as you might have done in the past leading to the dissatisfaction of the people at work. If this card has appeared in your reading then it means that this is already happening in your life or is soon going to happen. You must start working in order to fulfil all the job requirements.

This card also shows that people at your workplace might not be impressed with you they might be collectively criticizing and demoralizing you which now you might start noticing and feel about it. This might make you think like quitting your job or career; but if this is your career that you love then you only need to persist and work harder. People that are not pleased today will run after you tomorrow if one of your formulas works.

If your question is about success of any endeavour then this card shows failure of it or delay in the fame you are expecting.

Seven of Wands

Keywords - Safeguarding, building a wall, fear, stopping

Appearance

This card appears with a man holding a wand in his hands against wands that are standing in his way, the expression is of anger or rebellion. There is a stream of water that is running down, which also shows that this man is trying to stop the water from flowing away.

Meaning

This card shows that there are things flowing into your life already that you now want to stop, you don't want to let go of something that you don't want to keep flowing; you were a different person when you started on this path but now circumstances are different with your level of success flowing. Signified by the water flowing away, you might be feeling the need to put a check on the emotions flowing or money or resources flowing in a particular direction; you might want to focus on your work and career as your emotions or relationships might be draining off your energy and focus.

There are obstacles in your path lying since long time, you might be knowing this too; but now you have decided to take action to remove them. Or you may already have started removing them. These might be physical obstacles in your life, there may be some people proving to be obstacles in your progress or there might be some things in your life that are proving as obstacles; this can be some furniture or clutter. You might also want to clear off some shelves in your wardrobe or office desk. If you haven't decided to do this, then you need to do it if you are feeling too chaotic while at work.

There might be some restrictions put on you by people who are frustrating you and now you want to remove them and start keeping those people at bay as they are blocking your life's flow. Or if you have people around you who are being obstacles then this card says you need to discard them from your life NOW.

As you can see the person has two different shoes, this card also shows that you must to be too engrossed in your work and progress that certain things that need attention are being over-looked.

Reverse

The reverse of this card says you need to take a stand against some things that are nagging you, but you are too out of the world or depressed or lacking the enthusiasm or fire to do it. You seem to let people tread on your feet and come into your space.

Your enthusiasm or fighting spirit for your work and career are missing, this might not be the right career that you wish. Or this space might not be pleasing to you. You might have exhausted yourself too much that your creative zing and the fire to keep rocking the show are now missing. Take necessary measures. See for accompanying cards for any serious health issues.

You might have been realized your naivety and feeling down due to it so much that the current problems that need addressing are going unnoticed.

This might also show that you might have given up your fighting spirit because you feel your opponents or competitors are too superior to you, and you would never match up to their standards. Feeling low, low self-esteem.

Eight of Wands

Keywords - Communication, media, speed, pace

Appearance

This card shows eight wands having a flight in air; they are freely released to help take up speed and save time. This quality is usually seen in our communication media where news reaches speedily, any other media that is based on communication like the internet, all are signified by this card.

Meaning

This card shows speed and pace in your life. If your life was slow or medium paced this card shows great speed entering your life. You need to deal with things fast, you might be very slow at your work or taking life as it comes. But this card shows that you have now to take speedy actions, take wise but quick action to make your work or career progress.

This card also is a card that signifies media the news, communication media, the internet and might be pointing out towards a career in this field. If you are already in this career then this card might be pointing out to quicken your plans and increase your pace with which you are dealing it with. This card might point out towards people in your life who are involved in this career.

This card might also ask you to *connect* to people that might help you in your career, or build new contacts that you help you progress in your field. Your creativity would prosper more when you increase your knowledge, and connecting with people from your field will help you gain more knowledge.

Also this card shows moving wands, so in every case it shows a 'movement' happening in your life. If your life appeared still or slow this will bring movement or you might have already started noticing it. The card shows 'you' making the movement, nothing would happen magically! In order for you to progress it's you who has to take charge and make the move. Always being on the move and working productively will help you to succeed quickly.

This card shows communication of all kinds, if you are not a good talker this card shows that you should talk more effectively and often to broaden your prospects for career and work. It also shows a job at communication media waiting.

Reverse

This card reversed shows that you might be too hasty in your work and decisions, not to take decisions where you haven't given a thought and not to act out on plans that are not well planned or organized. You might incur losses if you act out hastily.

Haste makes Waste; this card reverse says this aloud. And warns you to keep check of your actions. Be moderately paced, plan out your actions well and act wisely.

This card may also show that you are too slow in your actions, and your slow life is not leading you to any progress. It actually is affecting your progress and leading you to more failure. It is making your life blocked and stagnant in one place. You need to keep moving in order to stay updated with today's world. This can also show such a phase coming up in your life where you might have to slow down and be stagnant. Also see cards around this card for further clearance.

This card reversed also shows that you might be weak at communication with others or the communication channels with people might go weak for a while in your life. This also is a way of life and we progress with each stumbling block in our life. Perhaps you need to build a strong relationship with yourself.

This also might show a weak communication with one's will, you don't communicate or listen to your will; and this is making your life slow or stagnant.

Nine of Wands

Keywords- insecurity, fears, panic, safeguard, shielding

Appearance

This card appears with a man standing and he has wall of wands lined together, this appears as if he has built the wall to protect himself. Further, it also points out somewhere that he is scared somewhere inside and so has done this.

There is a mountainous area behind him which shows he might be scared of uncertainty.

Meaning

This card coming up in your reading shows that you are scared of something or you were scared of something in your past due to which you have built a wall where people cannot reach you, just so that they cannot harm you. You might have already seen tough times or perhaps injured or hurt in these circumstances. This is why you have built the protective wall. But this might no longer be the case, in present there doesn't seem any danger beyond the wands and so it shows that there is no danger in the present. You have just made this as a place for you to feel safe. This wall might be now creating problems for you to 'open up' and mix with people.

Your emotional wounds or physical problems in the past might have made you too cautious or precautious. You scare at even the drop of a pin and examine each and every grain of sand that comes to you. You need to let go off this attitude of yours. It is just blocking your progress.

This also shows that your fears and panic have blocked your creative abilities such that you cannot act freely whenever you want. This might be also pointing out that you are missing out prospects for your career or opportunities for improving your abilities.

This also shows insecurity and doubts or distrust towards oneself. When something external is dangerous your shield can protect you, but when you are afraid of your own decisions, dreams, or thought pattern than who is going to help you? You need to trust yourself. Trusting ourselves itself builds a layer around us to help us protect from outside dangers.

You might he tired, worn-out and in a terrible condition yet you protect yourself and are standing your grounds just so that your task completes. This card also asks you to be more steadfast.

Reverse

The reverse of this card shows that you might be endangered but you don't feel this or care about this and so walk about freely. It also shows that you don't even carry necessary precautions when needed. You might fall into danger sometimes.

You also might be surrounded by some hidden dangers either from people or the environment around you that are not appearing right now, but you are susceptible to get hurt by them.

This card might also show your destructive nature that you have developed, you already might be having health problems yet you don't care about it and are going into more such situations that would hurt you.

You might give up at the last moment when you are about to win, just wait and have a little more patience.

You might be panicking in vain; you might have forgotten to build safety for you.

Also don't forget to check regularly as to all your important work related things are safe or not.

Ten of Wands

Keywords - Working hard, work load, career at fullest, persistence

Appearance

This card appears with a man trying to life 10 wands, his stature looks like lifting them is too much for him and he is bending down due to the weight. There are buildings appearing far away and this shows that this man would have to carry these logs too far away. The distance seems long, but the determination seems strong. It feels it's tough but he would carry it off till there.

Meaning

This card shows lot of hard work and persistence. You need to dedicate lot of your energy and time to do this much work. This cards showing up says that you are on this track and have taken up a lot of work, you might be doubtful whether you would be able to complete it or not; but this card signals that though it's tough you need to put your faith in yourself and you would be able to complete it.

This card also shows that you might be getting this much work in the future, of course if this card falls in the future position; and also near future if this card falls elsewhere in the coming time or present position of the spread. If this card is in the present position then you need to take up work, perhaps you need to take your job or career seriously and start working for improving quality of your life in the future.

This also might show a bit of laziness that you might be having, and not taking up work according to your capability. You might be seeing that the work is to be done for quite a long time and it's too much work indeed. But when this workload lies in front of you then obviously it is you who will have to do it.

This also shows a potentially high-level goal or ambition that would make others feel you might feel pressure doing it, but you think too far into the future and feel this is the right thing to do for you. You must go ahead and start doing this work!

This card also shows that you have taken up much work, but don't forget to keep looking forward and checking your priorities. This man in the card cannot see on the road as his vision is obstructed by the wooden logs, but he needs to see the way clearly or he would fall down. Same way you too need to see your way clearly or your near future or there may be chances that your work would go in vain.

Reverse

The reverse of this card shows that you have taken up too much work, which you ought not to do; you feel stressed doing it. The work you are doing isn't required to be done with this much stress or priority.

You taking too much work, is harming your health, you might be having back problems. Stop working, where you might need to put stress on your back area.

This card reversed also shows that you are too obsessed to work hard. There may not be any need or current requirement at your workplace to do this; yet you indulge into this much extra work. Perhaps this might be showing your other drawbacks. You might want to shun other important responsibilities or escape other meetings. This card might point out towards you or other people around you doing this.

This might show that you have a long way to go with this much burden of work, but you have already given up due to the lack of will-power to carry out the work. Whether you agree or not but you will have to finish the work that's thrusted upon you.

Page of Wands

Keywords - Enthusiasm, passion about to flow, creative thoughts

Personality

This person would be of medium to tall height, with an athletic build, not too weighty and neither too slim. Skin can be peachy coloured to all medium tones. They are centred people looking quite calm but an ocean of creativity to learn something new, to discover something new runs within.

Appearance

This page appears with a wand that is his discovering stick, he stands amidst barren lands, and his mind seems at the peaks of thoughts of creating or producing something. He holds the stick with both his hands. His robe has images of lizards which are a symbol of creation. A lizard regenerates a new tail when it is destroyed. So this energy is infused in the page too.

Meaning

The page of wands is a person who is lively, agile and ambitious in nature. They are also on the verge of creating something. They would never sit idle, if they ever do then they are thinking of creating something new. Same thing appears here, this page is standing and his look appears quit thoughtful; and he is actually having huge ideas and schemes cooking in his mind at this stage too. He is surrounded by only barren lands yet his mind is thinking of ideas to create something.

The robes have the image of a lizard on it; lizards have the capability of regenerating their tail on their own if destroyed; which here signifies that the Page is also infused with such creative energy. The barren lands can also hold the capacity of holding a creation that is worthwhile.

Page of Wands hold the capacity of thinking and coming out with ideas that are very brilliant and productive at the worst of times or situations, these can be trusted upon.

If not a person this card signifies ideas of creating or producing something new out of nothing.

Reversed

Reversed this card shows a person who is very confused with what he wants, he might be up with an idea at a moment and at the next moment he isn't interested in that idea. He is very much small minded, cannot keep his word. He keeps jumping from one idea to another without giving it results, just a mere idea popper.

Confusing, frustrating, negative thoughts and ideas running out of control in one's mind. Person feels maddening, also blocked what to do next as not clear with any one thought.

You might have bought on others thoughts and ideas as your own, this might be causing confusion. Other's minds are more powerful than yours resulting into you appearing indecisive at peak moments to take decisions and then others decide for you. You letting others decide for you, implementing only what others think is good and innovative is now disturbing your abilities as you cannot work on your own thoughts.

You need to put a halt to "listening to only what others have to say" and "doing what others feel is right for you", "thinking in a way others feel, must be your thought pattern" and start working with your mind independently. You can start with little things that give pleasure to you; which would help you to uncover the full power of your mind.

Knight of Wands

Keywords - Pace in career, speedy success, passion, ambition, dreams come true

Personality

This person is a fiery-natured person who wants his dreams to come true at all costs, he is ready to devote time, energy and persists till he gets what he wants. He can work 24 × 7 for the fulfilment of his dream, he's an athletically built charismatic person that draws attention wherever he passes. A warm hearted, affectionate person; medium-tall and well built, with earthy skin tones.

Appearance

This knight appears with a fiery look on his face; his eyes are focused on his goals. He holds the wand and charges right into the eye of his targets. He is accompanied with an equally charged Horse. The knight has worn a garb which has lizards drawn on it. Lizards have the power of regenerating their own body parts the same way this knight has the power to regenerate his energies until he finishes off his work completely.

Meaning

The work at hand need to be put into action right now, you might be having second thoughts about your plans but this card says you need to put them to action right now, this can be your career or work related plans. These can also be your goals that you have decided for your life. If this card appears when you are wondering when to start working on your life plan then this card has hit at the right moment; you need to start working right now for your life plans.

He will be having dreams to achieve that are quite higher than what his abilities or personality seems, but he has the desperation in him to fulfil them. He has the will to do it; he also has the daring to do it. He never thinks that he might lose or fail. He always has a back-up plan ready if that ever happens. He is a go-getter. While all the others in his group have fun and party his mind plans out his career and projects. He though is not a boring kind of person, he is a charismatic person.

He also cannot accept no for an answer he would get upset soon, but to cover up that effect he would come up with an even better plan.

This card also shows career and work at their heights, you may have to work more or faster to help keep the pace at your job space. Though this card promises a steady pace, you also need to focus on only the targets that you have to achieve. This card might point on focusing on one work at a time.

Reversed

When reversed this card shows a lack of pace in all your undertakings. This card may also show lack of initiation power, you might be having all the resources but the will-power or the confidence to start something new might be missing.

Your attention might be caught by many options and you might be losing focus due to it. Select one particular job at a time and put all your energies at it. You need to keep yourself focused until your goal is fulfilled.

You might be losing interest or the drive that you initially felt at the thought of the plan, and now when you have decided to initiate it with all the requirements ready you don't feel like going forward with it.

This card also shows lack of persistence in you. If you feel this card doesn't signify any personality in you then this might show the situation in your life when you are not able to put things into action.

Queen of Wands

Keywords - Artistic, friendly, tough, articulate

Personality

This female has a tough athletic body; she is a warm & affectionate person with tough looks. She believes in the here and now. She is friendly, believes in building faith in people. There's no task that's tough for her. She is career minded at the same time is a very good human being.

Appearance

This card appears with the queen seated on a throne, she has a sunflower in hand; which means she loves to greet people with love and freshness. On the other hand she also holds a wand which shows her strictness when she demands work. There are lions on both her arm rests which show her ruling capability. There are also lions drawn on her throne that are shown shaking hands which means she can even bring two lions together in a forest. There is a black cat at her feet which means she thinks with a broader perspective and wants to break old rules that are just humbug. On one side there is water and on the other side is land, means she is balanced with her emotions and the materialistic world.

Meaning

This person is a middle-aged female/male with qualities like passion, compassion, love, mercy, steadfastness, believer in truth, spreader of love and happiness, can make anything possible, in them. They are athletic built but are quite loving people despite of their tough looks.

This person can work for long hours; they are probably at higher posts in their work. They have already achieved a good position in their career and strive to keep improving it. They are also the go-getters like the other two personalities in this suit but she knows to be a human at the same time. She never forces her employees beyond what they can do.

She always likes to think different than the normal crowd. Her house would also be decorated with something different than the conventional way. She likes to break all old rules that work no more and loves to surprise people with her doing so.

She is quite a balanced person; she loves to slowly reveal her brilliant thoughts after everyone around her settles down. She loves to consider everyone alike.

If this card doesn't signify any person then this card signifies a situation you are in at present; at times when you need to break off old beliefs and walk ahead. Bring equality and friendliness wherever you go. You need to start getting into the leading position, and bring law and order. Situation where things are handled very carefully and people are taken care of.

Reversed

This card when reversed shows a person who has majority of manipulative ways to bring out things/resources for/according to them. They are very smart in talking out things. They would do anything to flee away from their responsibilities and not do their work. They are someone who doesn't like to work but yet likes to have all the comforts in their life. They would do anything to get these luxuries in life.

They are not at all loving or caring they actually have qualities where they might be repelling people away from them due to their nature. They don't like socializing at all and prefer to stay quiet in a corner when forced to get out into the society.

If this card doesn't show a personality in the reading then it shows lack of love and charm in your surroundings. There may also be an unfriendly atmosphere where nothing seems to be going bad and yet people are not at all comfortable in this environment.

There may be myths and orthodox thinking that might be prevailing at this point of time. This needs to be got rid of.

King of Wands

Keywords - Patient listener, hard to escape, work is worship.

Personality

A moderately tall, athletic built person, this person is of peachy-wheatish coloured skin tone. They are tough looking with a soft heart. They have love for their work and goals inbuilt in them. They like to reward people for doing their work; they are entrepreneurs, bosses, and CEO's of huge organizations.

Appearance

This king is seen seated on a throne from the right side. He has a wand in his hand, his expression shows he is listening or understanding something. The wand in hand shows his strictness where his work is concerned. There is shown a lizard on his robe as well as on his throne, which is shown eating its own tail. The power or regeneration is present, at the same its shown tail being chewed off continuously which shows creative energy is never put at rest, continuous flow of creative energy.

Meaning

This person is a born leader, leadership qualities, steadfastness, humility, achiever; he is a person who has already achieved a great deal in his life; he maybe an owner or entrepreneur of an organization. He bursts with creativity and wants to reach more and more heights in his career.

This person is one who has achieved something in his life, usually of the type where they go from rags to riches by their own hard work. They have brought their dreams to fulfilment by their own toil. They have now achieved a top post but still keep striving to become better and better at their work. They are the bosses but they don't have that pride even a bit. They like to compete with sheer talent, and praise when they come across some really talented people. They like to know and understand people and their talents such that they can use their abilities fully at work and help people to bring the hidden magic in them.

This person has the capacity to keep generating creative ideas continuously. They seem like geniuses who keep giving out breakthroughs.

If not a person then this card shows that you need to build a status like this king in your society. You have qualities of an entrepreneur, a leader, a boss; turn your dreams into reality and keep moving forward in life.

Reversed

Reversed this king is an unsuccessful person, a middle-aged or elderly person who just talks big about ideas wants a big life but never keeps his promises or never works his way out to what he says. As we say man doesn't say what he talks of just like thundering clouds don't always rain.

He is a lazy, good-for-nothing man who tries to shirk his responsibilities. Whenever work for him is put aside he would vanish out of that situation, and would appear after making sure that work is already done.

This man is well known in the society for all the bad qualities he has. He has an unending supply of ideas where he can shun his duties. He also doesn't take any responsibility in his family. He would never be present at family events due to workload involved. At work he might have gambled so much of money from all sources that people don't trust him for lending money.

If this card doesn't show and person then it shows that a phase in life where you are not in a career or work place which you don't like. This place might be completely out of subject to your interests, or people might be quite bossy.

Suit of Cups

Love is the most awaited and most desirable energy in our life. Suit of cups stands for the Love energy. As the quality of water to be considered healthy when flowing, same is with us; when Love energy keep flowing towards us and from us to the world then the flow of our life stays healthy.

And of course this is not possible every time in our lives. When the Love energy flow is blocked or altered in any way then problems arise in our lives. Love is the sole energy that holds this entire creation and so when we feel devoid of it our entire being screams out for it to come back.

Love energy feels as if second to our skin but yet ALL OF IT isn't understood by us. We need to learn, develop, and become flexible for accepting it throughout our lives. The infinite energy of the creator comes in little lessons throughout our lives. And only that's how we learn about its vastness fully.

Learn about this suit here; learn how to bring back balance of giving and receiving Love energy in your life through this suit of Cups.

Also this suit is of Love and Love energy is the eternal energy for healing and rejuvenation so this suit also signifies healing and speedy recovery.

Ace of Cups

Keywords - Love energy enters, new relationship, gift of love

Appearance

This card appears with a hand coming out of nowhere and offering a cup, the cups stand for relationships, love, healing, and affection. There are five streams pouring out from the cup, and a bird is seen putting a coin with a cross mark on it, into the cup. There are lotuses in the pond below.

Meaning

The card means a new cup or emotional relationship is about to enter into your life. This can be a love relationship, a new affectionate friendship, a wish come true or new love and affection energy pouring into existing relationship. This relationship can be between anyone, it can be within family members, friends, affectionate colleagues at work.

As this card is a card of love, and the cup is shown offered this card can also be an offering of love, i.e. birth of a new soul.

The appearing of this card shows that your life is about to change there is a new spark of love entering into your life. This would change your life completely.

This also shows a time in your life where you feel the need to give out your love the most. You would like to give your love through emotions, gestures, gifts, presents etc. But the more you give the more you would feel the need to give more. You are at your emotional best at this time. Also if you are not giving out love or expressing love freely then the appearance of this card says that you need to do it at this point in your life.

Also if for long if you had been thinking of gifting your beloved/friend/family/other people with something then take this card as a signal to do it ASAP.

The card also signifies a new spark or motivation entering into your life resulting into speedy recovery from any illness.

Reversed

When reversed this card shows a blockage of Love energy in your life. You are blocking love energy from entering into your life. This may be because you might have made past mistakes or seen failures in love relationship. And so now you try blocking out this energy so that you don't feel more hurt. But when this card is reversed it says that due to this attitude you are missing out something good in your life. You might be having really loving people around you who want to share their love with you. But you avoiding it is hurting them and driving them away. You need to forgive yourself for past mistakes and give yourself another chance to give and receive love in your life.

This card also shows that you might want to get into a relationship with someone but there is delay in it or the other person isn't ready for it right now. They might be in another relationship or may not be able to decide it for you.

There also might be problems in other relationships like between members of family, friends or between colleagues. Things won't be messy but still everything won't feel right. Either you or other member might be having problems opening up.

You also might feel relationships that are just a formality; life would be feeling old and boring. No new spark or energy; just old people, old routine and sometimes just formal exchanges of loving words and expressions.

Two of Cups

Keywords - Partners, soul mates, friendship, new partnership.

Appearance

This card appears with two figures coming close to each other and offering each other a cup, there is an angel in between them with a lion's face, and the caduceus symbol. They both have a tiara worn on their heads, one of flower and other of leaves; as flower and leaves cannot be separate they are part of the same plant same way these two people are like one soul two bodies. There is a house seen in distance also meaning stable family life or building up a new family.

Meaning

This card shows a new relationship beginning, love relationship that where there in immense exchange of affection and care. This new relation is a gift from the divine and your relationship is protected against all odds.

This card also shows a new friendship budding or a new business partnership that is not just professional but the two people involved are emotionally bonded to each other. The pic shows a male and a female but reality might also show relationship between either two males or females who might be good friends or business partners.

The relationship that might be flowering might be either of lovers, or love between family members, friends, colleagues. It can also show accidentally bumping into someone strange to you with whom you would develop an affectionate relationship.

This also shows giving and receiving of love or any gifts in a loving relationship.

The card also is a sign of balance and harmony entering into your life. The male and female forces flowing into our body, the yin/yang is balanced as signified by this card; which brings good health physically, mentally and spiritually.

The two people are also shown standing at quite a distance; this shows that this maybe the beginning of any relationship where the two people haven't yet developed the comfort level for each other, the ice is not yet broken. Yet their feelings are deep and wish to share their deepest feelings with each other.

The house in the background signifies an addition of a member to your family, perhaps you or your kids might have found a life partner. Or it may also signify you to start thinking in this direction.

Reversed

The reverse of this card shows that there may be distance between two people who are ought to come closer. Perhaps a relationship that is forcefully built or built because of compromise is not letting these two people gel with each other well.

This card also might signify the beginning of distance forming in an important relationship. You might have to give yourself time for this relationship. Perhaps not giving time and attention to it is making this happen. This relationship can be between anyone your partner, family, friends, or business partners.

The caduceus being the symbol of healing when appears reverse in this card shows that there may not be proper healing happening mentally, physically or spiritually. This may take time. Healing is slow. You might be making yourself of devoid of love in some way which is not allowing yourself to heal. Your soul needs love to help let flow the love energy into your body so that it heals quickly. Perhaps your relationship not working might be prolonging your illness or affecting your health.

This also shows conflicts in a family, two people may not be on good terms with each other and this might be resulting into problems within the family. Disharmony, imbalance and tipping of the scales too much on one side leading to feeling loveless, sad, and traumatic.

Three of Cups

Keywords - celebration, rejoicing, party, marriage, get-together

Appearance

This card appears with three women raising their cups out of joy, they have adorned their heads with flowers. There are also flowers and fruits around them. One of them holds a bunch of fruits. They seem to celebrate something.

Meaning

This card shows celebrations of any kind coming soon into your life. It can be a marriage, or a party; party for succeeding, getting promoted, engagement party, or the birth of a child. This card also depicts the birth of child as fruits are shown in the celebration. It can be a pre-birth or a post birth celebration.

This card brings immense happiness, joy, fun, laughter, togetherness, enjoyment into your life. It may show you already into such a situation or it can show such a time coming in shortly.

This card can also show forthcoming endeavours in any of you, this would lead to celebration. It would build a connection right from your hearts of all the people involved in it.

Flowers and fruits bring freshness and nourishment into our life. They provide immense nutrition and the upliftment of the mind, body and soul; which is depicted by them here in this card. You are already in this phase currently or about to step into such a joyful phase. This card shows fun, joy, happiness at its most in your life.

Reversed

This card shows a delay in any such celebration that might be scheduled. There might be a sudden delay or postponing in parties, engagement or wedding that might lead to frustration, stress and gloom. This card doesn't show out just because of luck. The celebration for which you were waiting has been put to a halt by the divine as you are not ready for it. It's always this reason and not anything else.

This can also show a miscarriage or an abortion.

This card may show a cancellation of a get-together due to unknown circumstances, or it may be because there were differences between people involved in it.

This card also shows that a group of people might be falling apart, maybe because of work prospects or because they no longer want to be in each other's company.

It can also show a break of marriage or engagement, or the breaking apart of a business.

It also shows that your overall health i.e. mind, body and soul is being undernourished because you don't allow yourself to enjoy, be happy and celebrate. You being aloof is your biggest drawback that is affecting your health now. Be open and mix with people to give and receive love, laughter and care.

Four of Cups

Keywords-Unacceptability, self-punishment, resentment, stubbornness

Appearance

This card appears with a hand appearing out of nowhere (a divine gift or offering) in front of the person who is seated under a tree and isn't accepting this gift. It's right in front of him so he of course knows that it's there.

Also there are three cups lying already in front of him, and they too are lined away from him.

Meaning

There are things coming to you, there are people, gifts, love and affection flowing towards you but you are not ready to accept them. You might be resenting towards something that might have happened to you in the past or you not having something that you really like. In this moment you are getting helping hand a gift from the divine and yet you are in a stage of non-acceptance. You need to accept what is coming your way freely rather than complaining over things/people you don't have with you.

There is greenery around the person, green colour is for the heart chakra which means there is immense healing love energy around you yet you are not ready to accept it. Any health conditions concerned for this spread would lead to prolongation of the ailment just because of you holding on to your stubbornness to not accept good things.

You at this stage might want something totally out of the blue; the things you require are always with you. But when you want something apart from these then you are out of the natural vibe and this will not help you. It would deteriorate your energies and vibes to quite a lower level and make your thinking small and narrow.

This also shows a person who has everything around him and yet not satisfied with what he has. He wants more or something different. Dissatisfaction, not being content are the two most messed up paths where anyone can lay. These paths will never allow you to be happy with what you have. Whatever you possess or however high you reach you wouldn't enjoy your success or life if you cannot accept what you are being given.

Our life has everything, every resource that we might need for our life's purpose; we will never be given anything more or less than that. If you are not happy with what the universe is offering you then you need to change your thinking or either build your life's plans high.

Reversed -

This card reversed says that you are accepting things as they come; you seem to be in a very light mood and are joyful with each grain of sand surrounding you. You need to take only those things that you really require and put away or let go of things that you won't need.

There may be certain things that you need not accept. There may be people who might be offering you with things you don't need or giving it off to you by force. You don't have to accept these things, and be stern about it.

When things, people, work is thrust upon you and not taken by your choice; you need to be careful as this might become a habit to the one who's offering it and when they get used to this habit it would be more difficult for you to say NO.

Say NO, whenever you feel like saying, say no to whatever you don't feel like having and say no to people you don't like being with.

Additionally you need to remove your focus from all that is attracting and shining in front of you and focus on things that you feel are right to do at that moment.

Five of Cups

Keywords - Crying, whining, loss, let go

Appearance

This card shows a man wearing a full black cloak, standing on a river bank and sobbing in his cloak. There are three cups fallen in front of him and two stand straight at his back. There is shown some liquid strewn around the fallen cups. The man seems to have not noticed the other two cups standing at his back. There is a bridge seen in the distance along with a building.

Meaning

This card shows that you are crying over people who have left you and gone away. These might be the ones who have made a mess in your life before going. You feel your world ending there and don't see any way out. You feel drained and deprived of love in your life as if those people were the only ones who loved you and cared about you. But you are missing something here, when you will turn around you will still find people/ friends who are still with you at this moment too. They are your strong supporters and real friends or family people who are with you in this tough time.

Don't cry over spilled milk. Stop whining at your trouble. Stop whining about people who left you. You still have caring people around you who care for you; if you don't take notice of them or care for them right now chances are that they too might leave you.

There is shown a bridge in the background which symbolizes that this is a time where you too have to act like this bridge. Let go of whatever wants to leave. You still have to stand firm on your grounds.

You might not be letting people go, relationships are not always long term. There are short-term relations too; when the purpose of any relation is completed the bond starts to fade. You need to understand this and let go people who want to leave your company.

After all love is not holding to people you like its setting them free. Binding people doesn't make them love us more. Doing this we block their life's flow as well as ours. To keep life flowing with harmony and peace we need to adapt to the changes that are happening naturally.

Reversed

This card when reversed might show that you are too insensitive or hard hearted; you are not at all bothered about people going out or leaving your life.

You might not want certain relationships and so would like to walk away from them. You need to think this really sensibly, this decision should not be a naive one neither it should be taken in a hurry. If you are certain that you don't want to stay in a relationship then you should be firm in it and walk away. There may be people who would sulk or try to stop you back but you need to keep going with what you have decided.

This card also shows that the situation of not letting go, crying and resentment has been surpassed. You have learnt the lesson you needed to learn from that experience and have moved on. Life has changed for you after you decided to let go of something that needed to go. You have decided to take new ways. To see your life's condition with a different perspective, to recognize and care for the people or things that still are with you and stand supporting you.

You have started making new friends and going out to new places, you are no more depressed and gloomy. This is the right way you have selected.

Six of Cups

Keywords - Sharing, giving love, meeting people, childhood memories, nostalgia

Appearance

This card appears with a boy and a girl shown on what seems like their house's compound, they are shown sharing or giving gifts or flowers to each other. Or it can be the boy who looks older is giving/helping the younger one. There are also more cups around them. They are near their homes and there is a guard seen at the back left.

Meaning

This card says that you must share what you have; it can be anything that you have in plenty. You can also give your love, affection and care to the ones who need it.

There might be people around you in your neighbourhood, who really need your love and support and a helping hand. These might not be people who are too needy but someone who might just need your love and care. Also this card appearing might point out that you is someone who doesn't socialize, you need to step out and breathe free in natural environment.

This card also demands building new friendship or improving your existing friendly bonds. It may be time for you to build a new relationship; this might prove to be your support in future. Or sometimes you can build a relationship just out of selflessness. Consider people needing your help like your friends, this may help them to open out better indirectly helping you more to serve them better.

There is also a guard shown in the background which means that you are in a guarded environment. There are only people whom you can trust. Tricky or doubtful people are kept away by your divine guards.

Flowers signify freshness entering your life and blooming and spreading fragrances, which here signify that your life would bloom with love and freshness and would start getting better and better with each passing moment.

Reversed

When reversed this card shows that you might be in an environment where building relationships or bonds with people around you; won't be safe for you. Additionally people around you might not be safe to hang out with.

This also can show that you might be helping, giving more of yourself then what the other person needs. You need to check with them, whether they need your help or not. Sometimes this card can also show help demanding people around, who would never get satisfied by any amount of help, resources or love you give. They would keep asking for more and more, making you feel drained out.

This card also might depict that there are people around you who need your help or support or love but you are being selfish and don't want to give the required. This would be your selfishness or your ignorance of it.

This card also might point out not to exceedingly love and care for the ones who don't care about you or the ones who are not wanting it/ demanding it. You might have been fixed in this turmoil of pleasing someone in a never ending way and they might not be noticing it or not needing it.

Seven of Cups

Keywords - Choices, options, dreaming, wishes

Appearance

This card appears with seven cups all containing different objects, one has a human face that says that this person might be wishing to have a friend or a partner, the one with a hidden face wanting surprises, a serpent wanting the serpent power, a castle indicating the need for a house or a better house, jewels for the wish to be rich, a wreath for the wish to become victorious, and a dragon for the desire of extra-ordinary abilities.

The cloud signifies that these are dreams; we can say castles built in the air.

Meaning

You are daydreaming too much, this may lead you to get disconnected from the 'now' and be in your dream world. You have to see dreams but then you have to come to the real world to turn them into reality. Just keeping on dreaming will not manifest anything.

There are many choices that you are having right now, and this is making you very happy. But the crucial point is that you are not sure which one out of them you need. This may lead to sweet confusion. The choices can be anything you like; it can be objects you love or people. In case of people you might create frustration amongst them as you are not choosing just one out of them all, you feel swept away by the feeling of having too many choices.

This card also shows that you are confused by the different opportunities emerging simultaneously from different areas of your life all at once. You are so much dazzled by this sudden outburst that you are not able to choose even a single task or object that might help you to move ahead one by one.

The card popping up in your reading also signifies that you may be much too involved in your day to day tasks that you have forgotten to dream your wish or visualize. Visualize your dreams as if they are real and dwell on that reality for a while; this helps to bring your wishes to fulfilment.

Reversed

The reverse of this card may show a lack of opportunities, when you feel you need them the most. Your condition might be such that you might be desperately searching for opportunities to emerge. But you find it your bad luck that none of them are emerging. Whatever happens is what nature has chosen for you, no it's not hard talk but its real talk. If opportunities are not coming your way you need to start building up something on your own. This may sound to be like a big challenge but this is the only option. When nothing appears around you, you can create one from within.

This card reversed also shows that you lack in the ability of dreaming, dreaming big and wild. Whatever we dream big is always achievable by us, it may appear impossible to others but we as the dreamers are always capable of achieving of what we have seen. "A person can only attain those dreams, which his eyes are able to see."

The reverse may also show that you might have been in a great depression, as you might be denying having good things in all major areas of your life. Your life may be ready to give you everything but you don't want to ask.

This also shows that you might be getting lot of surprises or choices or new things but you lack the 'want' of having them.

Eight of Cups

Keywords - Detachment, walking away, spiritual search

Appearance

This card appears with eight cups standing erect on the banks of a river, river depicting the harmony of emotions; and there is a man seen walking away from the cups and going to the mountains. Mountains since ancient times were the place of retreats for the ones seeking spirituality. There is the moon shown above which has two faces.

Meaning

This card directly shows that this person is not having any interests in a materialistic life or attachment to people, they rather like being alone and aloof from the common crowd.

This card also shows a need for spiritual growth, you need to connect to your inner self now rather than being out with the others and partying. You don't feel connected to anyone even if you are in a group, you need to go in search of the inner truth and know yourself better.

There may be lots of good things in your life, this may be all materialistic things/people you love and who care about you but none of them pleases you. You never find satisfaction with the love they are offering you, perhaps you don't feel you deserve that love and affection and move away from that situation as you feel suffocated. All that glitters isn't gold; you need to find what gives you real happiness and satisfaction and not just be happy with what others feel is good for everyone.

This card also shows that you need to give away some attachments in your life, there may be some relations some things or objects that you like but you feel that they are of no need to you now. They should be given away or should be left. You need to move ahead in life, and holding to things people that are no longer serving their purpose is leading to a blockage in your life. You need to keep the 'water' flowing. You emotions feel blocked when you don't do this. You might be feeling like leaving but you don't find any sensible reason to take off. Sometimes you don't need a reason for doing things that your heart feels right. When you do them only time tells what you have gained by doing that timely action.

This also shows that you might have to move out to a different place away from your loved ones.

Reversed

Reversed this card shows that you need to fulfil your duties in this current situation and only then move away from it. You leaving your duties half-done would lead to these people or situation turning back and knocking again and again at your doors.

This card reversed also shows that you are not comfortable with the people around you but still you are compelled to do it. Situations might be such that you won't have a different option to move on and neither do others have an option to move away.

This card reversed also shows that after a period of staying away from your loved ones you might once again get a chance to meet them, this might be a short visit or it might be a permanent shift.

This card might show that you are getting too attached to things and people and thus you are devoid of self-knowledge. You might be caring too much for others and you don't care for yourself at all.

Nine of Cups

Keywords - Pride, satisfaction, sit back, contentment, achievement

Appearance

This card appears with a middle-aged man sitting on a table. His clothes are simple and the in the back has 9 cups arranged. This man shows satisfaction of having achieved something, he might have worked hard for and now sits back and enjoys the fruit/rewards of it.

Meaning

You have achieved something after putting a lot of hard work and toil which would now yield good results. You will soon be getting equally rewarding fruits of your labour.

This card also shows the completion of a cycle as number nine suggests and getting the results of it. This is a cups card so this also might show the completion of a relationship based goal; you might have achieved love and affection from someone whom you liked and this card shows your feeling of satisfaction due to this.

This card also shows a bit of pride that this person might be having due to his achievements. Whenever pride takes over there is always a fall, you need to keep this in mind. Always keep trying to improve more and more on each level of your life rather than aiming to reach perfection. As perfection is a dead point, nobody can move beyond it. But bettering yourself at every moment will help you improve yourself by helping go beyond perfection.

This card also shows that by working hard daily you might have forgotten to sit back and rest; but when you achieve your results it's time for you to sit back and enjoy the rewards of your success.

Time to sit and relax, this also might show a time where you could take a small holiday and spend some quality time with your family. If it's not possible then try to spend some quality time with yourself.

Reversed

Reverse of this card shows a restless time, you might need to need to rush at a time where you felt a sigh of relief. Situations arise suddenly that would make you run on the tips of your toes. Restlessness might arise. This also shows the restless feeling within you that might be making you feel this way. There is no outer circumstance that would give rise to such a feeling, it lies within you.

Your achievements or your progress might turn upside down, all your hard work and toil might appear to go in vain and plans would fail or your already achieved results of success might get washed out, giving you sudden trauma and rage. Keep calm, you cannot move back after reaching so far.

This card when reversed shows that you might be having a discontentment feeling that prevails all the time. You might be doing everything to get success but still achieving that success might not give you that level of satisfaction, with the kind of hard work you put in.

You might not put in much of hard work or labour for the things you wish to achieve but you still want to reach a highly aimed stage. Hard work only can bring you to the level you are dreaming of. Dreaming about high goals and then working to bring them true would bring you true satisfaction.

Ten of Cups

Keywords - Joy, completeness, family happiness

Appearance

This card appears with a man and his wife as we can assume, there are two kids playing next to them. There are ten cups in the sky; there is a house in the background. The stream of water, as it's a cups suit shows emotional flow here.

This couple is very happy with the kind of life they are having.

Meaning

This card shows balance and harmony in your family life. You are deeply satisfied and joyful about the kind of bond each member of your family shares. A sense of well-being and security to have each other flows among every member of your family. This might have already started happening or is soon to happen to you.

This card also shows that you are about to enter into a family life of your own, this card might show a marriage. Moving into a house of your own with your spouse is also signified by this card, the literal indication of having a 'family'. You might have started thinking lately to have a house of your own; this card acts as a green signal to put that thought into action.

This card also shows childbirth, or it may show one more addition to your family.

This also shows a short vacation out with the family.

This card also might be a signal of dream fulfilment. This scene might be your dream to have a house by a river or seaside and two kids, and living happily with your partner and kids.

Reversed

When reversed this card shows a disturbance or disharmony to a well-balanced family life. This might be minor or may cause major changes. Family members might not want to stay below the same roof and family might split.

This card also shows a family bonded together materialistically; but from within, there may be differences among people. If there are no differences, then there may be a lack of warmth between members of the family.

This also shows a disharmony amongst people you love and care for having a disagreement on thoughts; this can be friends staying together or colleagues working under the same 'roof'.

From a higher point of view this card could show your disharmony with your inner self, a turn away from your real home (your core being or God). This card reversed might show that with the amount of dissatisfaction you are observing right now you need to still keep faith in yourself and support yourself at this time.

Page of Cups

Keywords - New thought for love, new idea about love life

Personality

This might be a young person or child who is very sensitive, loving, and caring in nature. Caring and affectionate, they win hearts with their talks. Fair to wheatish and fair complexioned. They can also be dark complexioned but having the same qualities about love as above.

Appearance

This card appears with a boy holding a cup in his hands; he is wearing a flowery outfit giving an impression about his soft caring nature leaving trails in people's hearts. Also there is water in the background showing the free flowing emotions of this person's life, or in life in general. Also the turban on the boys head suggest a steady minded person but very emotional.

Meaning

This card shows a person like this in your life, or it can signify yourself. You are a person who is very sensitive, the turban shows the thoughts and mind are steady and focused but the Flowing River at the rear shows an outburst of emotions all the time. You may be very emotional and get touched by almost any little thing around. You get sad looking at the sight of any creature hurt or anything destroyed and create a huge matter about it. You need to balance your emotional side and use it as your strength.

This person can be anyone of young age, this card shows the inability of handling emotions. This quality can be found in an individual of any age, it can also show an elderly person who is very sensitive and cannot handle emotional situations well.

This can also be a situation or a phase of your life where emotions would be flowing freely and sometimes in an uncontrolled manner. And this card acts as a signal that you must control your emotions like the tightly tied turban that signifies a steady mind.

Reversed

When reversed this card shows emotional turmoil, there may be emotional crisis this person is going through, or it may be you who is going through such a time. You might be feeling out of touch due to lack of good feelings.

Also this card says that this person is quite an emotional person and sensitive, this person might be hurt due to uncaring people around him. He just needs a little tender love and care and all his chaos would stop.

This card also points out to person lacking sensitivity or caring for people, they maybe rash and brute.

Knight of Cups

Keywords - Passion, romantic, affectionate, caring

Personality

The knight is a person with a drive of passion to live his dream. He wishes something and then works towards fulfilling it. He is much passionate about it.

Appearance

This card appears with a Knight seated on a horse with a cup in his hands. His hand with the cup is raised, he is in a strange land where there are no houses seen and there is a stream of river flowing in the background. The river signifies the flow of emotions. Also this card depicts that the knight is driven by his emotions.

Meaning

The Knight of Cups is a person who is passionate and active. He is always driven by his dreams. He wishes for things and gets completely swept away by it; his dreams, passions, wishes of the heart are what drives him. He is an emotional person with the zeal to always go the way of his heart.

He takes everything to be true; he wears his heart on his sleeve and thinks people too are that way, and gets driven to them.

Affectionate, loving, caring, always takes the first move, never neglects others who talk straight from the heart, and is friends with everyone who like to talk to him.

He has a soft corner for every big and small being. It is this person who is always in love with something or the other. He is in love with just everything around him. A very few people display these qualities. They are charismatic and attractive due to their loving nature. He always listens to his heart and decides according to it. He trusts his will rather than anyone else. It can be you yourself as this person or someone around you who would be helpful to you in your situation. It can also be a soul mate if the card pops out in a relationship reading.

Also this card states that you need to listen to your heart and be ruled by your heart. You might be quite a tough person, but this card says that you should be soft, caring and affectionate. You can be tough at work time but be soft with yourself when you are not at work. Also treat people with affection.

Reversed

This card when reversed shows that the person concerned is rash, ruthless, and brutal towards himself as well as others. He doesn't take care of people around him and their feelings. This can be a male or a female who is acting this way, or it can be a person around the Querent who is behaving in this way. They may either behave in this way just so that the Querent leaves them or breaks their relationship or this person might not want to continue their relationship with you.

This card also shows that a person who is quite emotional, caring and loving might be under great pain and so changes their way of being affectionate towards all. They might turn totally opposite to what their positive side is. They might turn inwards, be quiet and unfriendly; won't bother about people if they ignore him.

Also this card shows that only listening to your head is not always good, you also have to listen to your heart. A good human being always is level headed with listening to his head and heart equally.

Also, this card shows that you might be too emotional and caring, giving too much of yourself to others. You might not be getting in return what you give out. This card advises that you should be good hearted only to the people who accept your goodness, leave others free who want to be their way.

Queen of Cups

Keywords - Nurturer, loving, compassionate

Personality

This queen is quite a loving person and caring. They would be very good persons probably the best kind of persons. They deal people with utter respect, hardly get hurt by anyone as people would never like to hurt anyone like them. They are usually healers, doctors and everyone else dealing with emotions and feelings.

Appearance

This card appears with a lady sitting near a riverside, water flows at her feet. She holds a cup in her hand as it's her achievement. She wears a white-coloured robe showing her peacefulness in nature. There is a baby inscribed on her throne which depicts that she is quite a nurturer and of motherly loving nature. There are baby merkids on the top of her throne again symbolizing her caring nature along with her feelings of being passionate. The cup she holds is felt she is happy achieving the cup i.e. the love of others.

Meaning

This person is a loving-natured person with a delicacy and passion that overflows. They are the saturated personalities of cups suit with the nurturing nature of a female. She acts true to herself, when she does that she also knows others who are doing it; can be very soothing or comforting person to talk to.

She holds a very powerful intuition and depends on it to guide her life as well as of people who ask her help. This card shows compassion, love, care, affection, intuition which is about to enter your life through a person or through circumstances. When this card signifies a person it could be a female middle aged or it can also rarely show a middle-aged man with these intense emotional qualities. When this situation strikes it is like an environment which is positively charged making you emotional. You might start developing the qualities of this card.

The card also shows intuitional development and developing of extra sensory powers. You might be signified by your guardians to do this as it is the best time for you to start developing your sixth sense. Nature gives us signals in the present what we will need in future, and undertaking those actions in present will help us to 'ready' for the future.

Reversed

When reversed this card shows a stone hearted, reckless, and un-loving person; such a person who hurts just every she comes across. She is a spiteful person who can never see good happening to others and will always try to poke her nose in every matter just to see the good others might be gaining. She carries this gloomy, gossipy nature that lowers the mood of everyone she goes to. She kind of knows this and enjoys this low-ness she carries to. Deep within this woman too is deeply hurt in her life, but she has chosen the negative path that helps her to stay away from her hurt self and just be comfortable with her present self.

This card also shows an emotional blockage of every kind. This card might bring a lot of emotional blocks as it is the highest emotional charge carrying and it is reversed which shows that this charge might get blocked or there might be an upcoming situation which would resultantly block your emotions to a large extent.

Intuitional feelings might be misdirected and cannot be depended upon in this situation. Your intuitions go wrong when you have scattered energies and a mind that's not focused or in your control.

King of Cups

Keywords - Balanced person, Focused, humble, compassionate

Personality

This is a quite humble looking person, his face drips with compassion and care, he is always ready to give a helping hand. A mature aged man with a heavy body, love for sweets, skin maybe fair to wheatish.

Appearance

This male appears sitting calmly on his throne with a cup in one hand and a wand-like object in other hand. This signifies emotions as well as creativity balanced in both his hands. The left hand where we take in energy has the wand which shows that he is full of creativity and gives out love to everyone he meets. He is shown sitting amidst a tumultuous ocean, yet his throne is still. There is a fish on the right shown jumping and a ship at his left which is steadily moving in this turbulent ocean.

Meaning

This king is a highly stable person and hardly shows that he is moved by anything or any situation. He is compassionate towards all, who are in trouble; but has the capacity of holding his calmness and not buy-on to others' disturbances; signified by the turbulent seas which are not harming the stability of his throne.

This king could be a doctor, healer, counsellor who needs to listen to the troubles of people and yet stay calm and be focused on his work. This person is usually like an agony aunt to whom everybody likes to turn to when faced with problems. Their calm composure sends out such vibes that people too learn to stay calm like him.

This male is the best among all males that anyone can have. He is calm minded and deals with everything with a cool mindedness. He never wants to rule but always wants to comfort people trusting in him because of his power.

This card when it doesn't show a real person then it might be showing a situation in your life. This situation might be somewhat disturbing to the world around you or the environment around you, but this card suggests that you should be calm and not get affected by this situation.

This also shows that there is this kind of person in your life who could be very easy going and compassionate. This person can be highly reliable and dependable. This card might be suggesting you to get more comfortable with him/her.

This card might also show that you need to balance your emotions as well as creative energy. You must be a very sensitive person yet you have to handle your emotions well and also at the same time balance your creative energies.

Reversed

When reversed this card shows a person who is imbalanced in his own self and cannot cope when terror strikes in his surroundings too. He is a controller not by force but by holding onto people with his emotional drama which actually is just a show off, he might not be the way he acts or expresses. His true nature can never be known as he changes colours with the changing environment but he may know very well how to catch hold of your weakness and control you. You need to get free of this man as he isn't trustworthy and dependable. Moreover he might be adding to your troubles as he himself cannot handle any of them.

This card also shows lack of balance between the creative and emotional sides resulting into a personality people cannot accept. When there is someone people are not accepting then the non-acceptance lies within those people too.

When not showing a person this card shows your environment which is quite unstable and you have to learn to achieve stability in this. Or you might need to get away from it. This also shows that the situation is completely manageable and can be dealt with if you have balance over your emotions and creative energy.

Suit of Pentacles

The suit of Pentacles represents the element Earth and takes the longest time to manifest as it has a physical form. The element of earth is connected to earthy energy, resources, money, property and belongings that are essential in our day to day life. It also represents the basic requirements of our physical existence like body, home/shelter, money, food.

This element is needed to be balanced in order to have a peaceful and fuller life. People who don't have this element balanced always have problems in their materialistic world and in some way or the other are suffering due to lack of resources.

The other three suits show their physical manifestations here. The thoughts take form of emotions, emotions motivate to take actions and actions bring out results in this physical world.

The people associated positively with this suit are the ones who are very successful in their physical world; they are successful at all levels.

Conversely, the people who are imbalanced somewhere in the other elements have scarcity in their physical dimensions.

This suit being the suit of materialistic life directly is connected to the working of your Root Chakra. This chakra when balanced gives you a balanced materialistic life where you have all the resources you need. And if this chakra goes imbalanced then the base of your life i.e. the materialistic world is shaken giving rise to imbalance in other suits too. If you want to help improve your materialistic life, then start using all the positive meanings of this suit.

Ace of Pentacles

Keywords - Opportunity to earn money, gaining money & resources

Appearance - This card appears like a hand appearing magically from a cloud like other aces in the Tarot deck. This stands for manifestation of any wish into physical form, or an opportunity that has come up to bring your plans to fruition. Also the garden shows the beauty coming into your materialistic life.

Meaning

You would be offered an opportunity that will help you to bring your plans or dreams into fruition. These plans can be anything emotional, financial, career wise or property wise. You will be offered an opportunity to help you manifest your plans into reality. This might also mean that the opportunity at hand is the one that will work out.

This card shows that your dreams or plans that you were working on till now have now come true and your wish is manifested in reality. This can also be a sign to let you know that the plans you have in your mind need to be put into action for quick manifestation.

The garden around ace of pentacles shows that your physical world or materialistic life is going to be beautiful. If you had problems in your materialistic life then this card promises an improvement in it. Also there is a path way shows coming into the garden, this might signify that you might get a way to make your physical world beautiful. Or if you already have some plan or idea then this might help you to make your world better.

This card also directly shows monetary gain in your life, you might find money coming to you in a very unusual way. This might be a source that would give you the money or offer a helping hand if you need monetary help.

This also shows a partnership at business, depicted by pentacle standing for 'money gain' through business partnership.

Reversed

When reversed this card means there is lack of money. You might also be lacking in resources that you need in day to day life. There also might be a need arising to borrow money from people. Additionally this shows loss of the resources you may have currently, either due to their damage or a giveaway as need for money.

This card also signifies that if you are wishing or planning for getting something into your life, then that may take some time to manifest or it may not manifest at all as the wish might be superfluous and maybe ill-planned or lacking planning. This also shows that opportunities that were coming your way have been delayed or taken on by someone else.

This card also shows failure. It shows lack of resources, inconvenience, and discomfort in your materialistic life.

This card also shows debt which is on-going or which is forthcoming. You might have to fulfil them sooner than expected or a huge unexpected debt is coming your way.

The physical world may appear awful and in chaos. Things might get filthier then what they were before. Work on your Root Chakra to balance out this situation.

Two of Pentacles

Keywords - Juggling, manifestation on a hold

Appearance

This card appears with a man juggling two pentacles in his hands, the pentacles form an infinite sign around them to show the infinite possibilities of the manifestation at hand. There are two ships in the background that are sailing in a turbulent sea which means there are difficulties yet they will be crossed.

Meaning

This card means that there are difficulties at present for turning your plans into reality, but you still should not give up, wait patiently and keep doing what is needed to help quicken up the pace for turning your dream into reality.

The ships in the background show that few things that you might need for your work are still 'stuck' somewhere, so till they don't arrive you have to manage with the resources at hand.

This card also signifies that the resources at hand are scarce so you need to keep them, and not let them go away right now. The figure is also looking a bit tensed due to this, but is still keeping the work on. So you too have to keep working even if you are stressed out or worried as your work continuation will help you to gain money or resources quickly.

"If you worry you cannot work, and if your work you need not worry"

The infinity sign also shows that there would be infinite opportunities for work or earning money coming your way. This also might be pointing out to still keep working on the current opportunity as only then will you keep getting more opportunities.

This card also says that the resources at hand money, land, property should not be dealt with right now. Don't give them off, even if you are going through a crisis, this card says keep these things with you. It also further pacifies you by the higher meaning that worries may come but you don't have to cloud yourself by them. Continue working in the direction you are right now.

Reversed

When reversed this card shows that you are not able to balance during odds that are coming up. You might miss the resources or money that you are holding at hand or you might lose the opportunity of gaining resources that are almost halfway from you.

This also shows that the goods, money or resources that you are expecting would be delayed causing frustration or may not reach you at all and might get caught up in confusion halfway.

This card also shows lack of opportunities to help you bring you the things you need in your life. Things may seem terribly worse as you feel that you cannot do anything while there is lack of money or resources.

This also shows that the path that you are planning might be very weary and result in a loss. You are advised not to take this path.

Three of Pentacles

Keywords - Orders, designing, focus on work

Appearance

This card appears with a man working and two other people showing him or directing how to work or maybe showing him the design of the work being done. It's a pentacle card so obviously shows physical work, getting in your shoes and working. It also shows some creative work done by hands, as shown in this card the man is carving pentacles into a wall.

Meaning

The card means getting into work where you might be taking directions from people and working according to their directions of choices of designs etc. This includes all kind of designing work, where people tell you what kind of work they want. This also includes engineers.

This card when seen in a different way, we also get a feel that people are ordering this man but he is completely focused on his work. This also can be the case where people nag you or criticize you, yet you should stay focused on your work and continue working as you are doing it.

The man's focus is completely on the work being done, also points out that if you are trying your hands on more than one thing, then this card says not to do so. Just work on one thing at a time. This way you'll be able to give justice to your work.

This card can be also pointing out towards careers where hands are used to work, like in civil engineering, boutique, fashion designing, salon, tattooing, etc.

This card also says that you should be in touch with the people who need your skills. When their work is done, yet keep asking for their feedback regarding past work and suggestions for other clients as well.

In a very literal way this card also points out to start serving at a cathedral. This might just not be church services but also other works involving the church.

Reversed

The card, when reversed shows weak focus and no attention on work at hand. You might be disillusioned and don't know what to do in life and so your work isn't pleasing you.

This card also shows that the work you have taken isn't what you call your dream job and so it isn't pleasing you.

This card appearing in your reading also shows that any work which involves physical labour too isn't meant for you, if this card turns out in a career reading.

This card also shows that you maybe too engrossed into gossiping or chit-chatting at your workplace which leaves your job undone, this card alerts you to start paying attention to your work more than the other non-productive activities at work.

This card also shows that you have ample work at hand, but you don't have any directions or training for how to do that work. This might also be intentionally done by your higher authorities who might be against you and wanting to degrade you when your work is not properly done.

Four of Pentacles

Keyword - Save money/resources, possessiveness, holding on, greed, and miser

Appearance

This card shows a man seated with two pentacles pressed under his feet, one held carefully in his hands, and one over his head. This man also is wearing a crown, which shows his high monetary status and yet being too miserly. There are shown many buildings behind him.

Meaning

This card means that you might be having ample of resources and are financially stable (signified by the crown) and yet you hoard on your money and resources. Which is making you miserly and you are not moving any further then that (as he's shown seated stable on the seat.)

This also shows that you are too possessive towards your belongings and also towards the people you love. This might drive the people away from you as people don't like it. Also this shows that you are too much with yourself, and you hardly open up shown by the folded hands across the chest; the whole world with a variety of people is waiting for you. You just need to go and embrace it.

This card also signifies that you might be having a lot of money or resources yet you need to hold on to them and use them wisely. There might be chances of getting losing them.

This card also shows greed for more, as this man sits in an anxious poise. He already has a lot with him that is all around him and which actually he needs to hide or put carefully yet he is looking out anxiously to get more.

This card also says that when you meet people, you should not part with your belongings and be watchful for them.

Reversed

When reversed this card shows that you need to protect your belongings which is not present in you. You might be very careless about your belongings; this may make you devoid of them. You might be having enough for yourself but you still don't have that much what we call abundance and so be careful dealing with your belongings.

This card also shows no interest in life, a sense of disconnection which makes your grip loosen with all things that you are possessing. This might make you lose important things and people in your life. You need to wake up and catch hold of all things important to you.

This also shows that the money you had saved or insured might be in danger and there might be chances of losing the money. This card can also point out to this situation in future and warn you to take action quickly.

This card also might signify not a good place for saving or investing money when you are building such plans and you find this card in your reading.

Five of Pentacles

Keywords - Poverty, lack, crisis, helplessness

Appearance

This card appears with two figures walking in the snow and who look as if they don't have any shelter. They look poorly dressed plus also not in a good state physically. Even in the cold climate and snowy weather they are forced to stay out which shows the clear lack of shelter.

Meaning

This card is the worst card for anyone that represents the materialistic dimension and lack in it. This card might show that you are having lack of resources in your life and sometimes it may also show lack of a house. To the worst situations in life this card points out to us, how off track we are from our life's purposes that we have made us devoid of all crucial resources in life.

This card also shows a lack or crisis of money in your life. It also may signify that you might need to go to borrow it from someone.

This card also shows that your physical body would be in a bad state. It can be of you or somebody close to you, and the situation altogether with your financial condition might be making it worse.

This card also points out to a shift or change of home. It can be at the worse time you've expected but the shift might be inevitable.

This card also might point out towards physical injury due to carelessness. It can be yours or someone around you who is important to you. Also see any court cards adjoining this card that may help to understand this person better.

Reversed

When reversed this card shows that a financial crisis that was worse and would have brought you on roads has just been escaped. You are no longer under any danger of this situation.

If you might be going through a crisis already and this card appears in your reading then this card assures you that this situation would be under control soon and the crisis would be lifted off.

This card also might show that moving to a place or shifting might get cancelled or prolonged.

You might be having a heavy heart changing places and this card shows that you won't have to make the shift.

This card also shows that if there was a situation of physical ill health then there might be an improvement in that situation and recovery would be speedy.

A card of crisis, and hardships and pain when reversed shows that these situations are either blocked from coming to you or are delayed. They might appear in future if you continue taking the wrong steps.

Six of Pentacles

Keywords - Donation, helping, giving

Appearance

This card shows a man who is giving money to people looking needy. This man might be having a lot and so is giving away very easily. Offering a helping hand is also depicted here, these people might be someone you know or someone who is a total stranger to you.

Meaning

The meaning of this card says that you have enough money that you can now start helping others. These people can be someone you know or might be total strangers.

This card also shows that if you feel someone needs your helping hand in some way, or needs help with resources then you can help them. If this reading is a query about the same then this card shows that you can surely give without any doubts.

This card also shows that this man might be a miserly or greedy person and might be hoarding money, and this card says to loosen your grip and let go of some money to give the needy too.

You may have people around you who might need help; they might be your neighbours or friends. You should help them as their demands are genuine.

This card also shows that you should give selflessly.

This card also shows that if you are in need of money then assistance will soon come to you. It can be either from some near ones or based on loan, which would help you to get out of this situation.

Reversed

The reverse of this card shows that you might be too selflessly giving away your money or resources and people might be taking advantage of you. You must help but not at the cost of you being taken advantage of. Be watchful and stop giving to people who don't need it any more.

Also this card shows that you are giving away easily but the people receiving it are now getting used to receive without working hard for it, and this is making them lazy and worthless. Set boundaries to giving money.

This also shows that you might be giving away too much money/ resources, which will make them scarce for you. So put a check on it and give, but also keep some for yourself.

This also might show a time where if you had taken money from someone in the past, then it would be the time to pay them back.

This also shows a time where you are advised not to donate or do any sort of charity.

People you feel need your help are not at all needing it.

Seven of Pentacles

Keywords - Waiting, investment

Appearance

This card appears with a man leaning on his stick near his crops, it seems he has planted his crops and now is watching over them just to protect them and also in a way of expecting getting returns from the crops. There is one pentacle at his feet, all else are growing which shows he has limited money until his crop reaps off.

Meaning

You have worked hard, put your skills in some project and completed it. Now is the time to wait patiently for it to grow and produce results. You must keep watching over it so that you can fulfil anything if needed urgently for the project.

Your money is put into safe investment and will take time to grow; you need to be patient and assured about it.

You have long-term plans that will help you reap abundant rewards in the future, you must work on them. When you are done with it, be patient as they will take some time to fructify.

This card also shows that if you were working on some plans/project since last few months, then now is the time when you will reap rewards from it. This card shows that success is confirmed and you will surely achieve the money that you were expecting from this.

The six of pentacles was for donating and giving others, whereas this card is a step ahead of it. This card says that you must save some for yourself too. Life's problems get solved on their own when we start caring for ourselves. The six of pentacles showed free flow of money but this card says that you have to save some money for yourself too.

There is nothing like selfless service, you can serve people better when you yourself are content by resources you have at hand.

Reversed

When reversed this card shows that this man is waiting and watching endlessly over something, which is not guaranteed that it will reap results. You might be wasting your time and energy after this.

If you are planning of investing money in something or partner up with some project that needs initial investment then you must not go for it, as this card reversed warns you that it would not come out as expected. You might lose your money or the project may be prolonged indefinitely.

Also this card shows that you are not doing any long term planning for yourself, neither investing for yourself that is going to be a problem. When this card appears in reversed then it shows you are vaguely deciding and working on short term plans without any distant or long-term visions. Everyone has to think and keep their future secure by some way of monetary investment or property investment. If you don't do it, you might be left with no sense of security in future.

This card also shows that you might be least worried about money and might be squandering it here and there, short-term thinking and no planning. There also might be hate or self-punishment towards oneself when a person doesn't want to see them happy in future. You need to work on the positive aspects of your life and think good about yourself in future and forgive yourself for the past.

Eight of Pentacles

Keywords - Self-employment, ability, skills

Appearance

This card appears with a man sitting and carving out pentacles; he has already made a few and is in process of making more of them. This card shows houses in the distance which might also point out to work far away from home. There seems to be no one around the man which shows he is working on his own with no one to instruct him.

Meaning

This card shows that a man is sitting down and doing his work by himself, the work done is by art of his hands and so this card points out to 'self-employment', or working with the art of your hands far away from your home.

If you are planning to get a store or workshop for yourself to work then this suit shows that you might get a place distant to your home. This also might be a blessing to you as it might help you to concentrate fully on your work, though you might feel the initial pain of being away from your home.

Also literally seeing this card shows working or studying somewhere in a distant land away from your home.

If you are looking out for a job or are planning which direction your career must go then this card shows that you must use the art of your own hands to do it. It can be anything that is done with hands.

This card also shows that you have to put in hard work for the project that you are working on. The man is seen engrossed completely in his work, and so you too have to be fully dedicated to it.

Also this card shows learning new skills and getting trained for it.

Reversed

When reversed this card shows that the work you have taken at hand might not be the right kind of work. You may not be having any precise skills in designing or using your hands to create something. Instead you may try your hands using creativity of your mind to become successful.

Also this card shows that there may be a lot of work pertaining yet you may not be motivated to do all of it. You might have got the grain of laziness in you, and the work that interested you till now isn't doing it anymore, and you are leaving it half-done maybe at the stage when it's almost done. You need to regain your interest in it and start working on it with the same passion you started with it.

This card also shows that the work you have taken at hand should be done one at a time. You might take 2-3 different workloads and try to do them with scattered effort. Whereas when you concentrate just on one thing at a time then you can put your wholesome effort in it.

This card also might show that you are lacking passion towards your work, you might be working away from your home and your mind just keeps wandering and worrying about people at your home. This may be getting in the way of your progress.

We are all part of a larger home and every one of us is taken care of at all times. And so you just need to proceed in your work, and complete it.

Nine of Pentacles

Keywords - Abundance, plenty, pleasures

Appearance

This card appears with a lady holding a bird, and walking in a garden. The garden has reaped a lot of grapes and there seems to be plenty coming from it. The lady is satisfied by the income she has as it is bringing all that she likes. She holds a pleasurable glance as if she is living the life of her dreams. There is seen a house in distance which looks quite posh and gives a feeling as if it is owned by this lady. There is also seen self-satisfaction from earning this for her.

Meaning

This card shows a time in your life when you have already put in the hard work, got the results and the rewards of your labour, and this is the time to sit back and enjoy your winnings. You feel extremely satisfied and happy about your achievements. If you have not achieved success yet then this card shows that you are nearing it and will soon reach this state.

This card also shows that you have achieved in plenty and now need to enjoy the rewards of it. If you have not got yourself any luxurious living equipment's then you must now get some and start indulging yourself.

When you work hard for some purpose day and night and put it your best efforts then it surely reaps good results. Your job is to also enjoy and accept all the results that you are getting. In the race of running behind working don't forget to enjoy the fruits of your labour.

The lush green garden and the posh house also might be indicating that these are soon to enter your life. If you are planning your future then this card says that you have to dream big and put up goals of having a huge palatial house.

As we can obviously see this card shows that this is a card of materialistic gain, abundance of money, rewarding time for your hard work. It also shows at the same time a relaxing and time to retreat and enjoy your rewards.

Reversed

The reversed of this card shows that your hard work that might have gained you huge rewards is not going to give you rewards as expected. The results might get postponed or not turn out as you wanted them to be.

Frustration, lack, and displeasure building up in your mind which might soon show up in your physical dimension too. You might be having troubles with self-acceptance or non-acceptance for your body or appearance. You need to start working towards it. Think only good about your physical body and your outer world.

Also this card shows that materialistic world might be turning out ugly. There may not be anything pleasing about it. You might be bored or unattached to or your outer world might have stopped pleasing you.

This card also shows that a huge amount of money might be needed to give away or parted with. It also shows all of a sudden events happening demanding spending of money.

This card also shows that you might not gain anything out of the work that you have done which may affect your confidence or passion for work but you need to not give up hope and start again afresh. Hope in your situation will help you keep the spirits up and gain motivation for working with the same passion.

Ten of Pentacles

Keywords - Richness, luxury, windfall, financial stability

Appearance

This card appears with a huge house, there are people seen smiling, there are animals as well in the house. People are wearing royal clothes which show richness in their life. There are two dogs that look tame, and there is also a kid seen. The people look happy and peaceful, giving a sense of self security this card brings. The man sitting looks as if he is reflecting back and recalling how he has achieved all of these for his family.

Meaning

This card shows that there is richness a windfall or a huge financial gain coming soon into your life. Either you are going to get this money from lotto or from a legacy. This also shows a heritage being passed on over to you. This might happen soon or might already be happening.

This card also shows that whatever job or work you have undertaken will see the sunrise of getting completed and reaching a result where they reap ample rewards.

This card shows a healthy and steady materialistic life where you have abundance and are secured. The sense of security that comes with a shelter, money at hand is seen here is about to enter in your life. Your hard work is finally going to pay off and put you in a place where there will be ample for just everyone around you.

This card also shows retirement, either yours of someone else's that might bring in a huge gain of money as well as sense of peace and satisfaction of the work done.

This card when shows up also depicts that any sort of money problems that you might be going through would end up soon and for good, you would never have to face such tough times again. This card assures money that is to stay with you and your family forever, at least until you need. Any debts or pending money will soon be solved and received. Debts will be paid off and also you will have the assurance of never needing to go under debt again.

Reversed

When reversed this card might show money going away from your house/ family. There might be the need to fulfil any debts that might be remaining or some sudden need to spend money arising.

Also this shows that any windfall or money gain that was coming your way is now being put off or getting cancelled. You might get disheartened by it. This might also be a conspiracy towards you to cheat away with the amount.

This card also shows financial insecurity pertaining to your family. There might be always the case, or your family might have started having this sense of insecurity maybe after a huge money loss or give away.

This card also shows that a huge sum of money might be needed to give away from your family money, maybe for the needs of the family. It might be a sudden need to spend money.

This card also shows loss of home shelter or property, leaving everyone insecure about future.

This might also show breaking and parting of the family after a conflict or due to lack of co-operation between members of the family.

Page of Pentacles

Keywords - New job opportunity, money growing ideas

Personality

This page has a personality of a very steady and quiet person; they are builders they will always try to build something or the other. This kid might show up interest in playing games that involves building blocks and alike. The child might have characteristics of being quiet and maybe too easy going and cool headed. But they are very good at persistence; they can keep working on something until it is finished.

Appearance

This card appears with a young boy holding a pentacle in hand, giving an idea he is offering something to us. The environment around him is lush green, there are fields shown in the distance which are not yet started to grow, giving us the rawness of this card. Only ideas are come up there is fertile land where you can sow them to get good results.

Meaning

This card means that there is a young child around you with these qualities. This child can be anyone in your house, maybe the youngest kid in the family. If you are an adult but still the youngest kid of your family then this card might also point out towards you, if you have these qualities.

This card also shows that there are ideas which have come up which might be of the type needing to bring something into manifestation into your physical life. The idea is yet not worked upon. But the appearance of this card shows that this idea is worth giving a try. You should plan it out and put it into action.

This card also asks you to stay grounded while you start working on your plans, as the seeds are yet to be sown and the crop still remains to grow. You cannot start dreaming high about the results, yes you have to plan out your vision but just dreaming isn't going to help. You need to steadily work on it.

This page can also represent an adult or anyone elder then that, the personality might be still of a young at heart and immature spirit who is high on dreaming yet still needs to learn the manifesting skills.

Reversed

When reversed this card shows that this person might be having too many ideas in mind, making it difficult to decide which one to work on. Or just that this might be a person already on the 7th sky and might be dropping vague ideas that won't fructify or ideas are such that are just thought for thinking, they are never intended to put into action.

Also this card shows lack of bright ideas, when you are in need of great ideas; you are just being devoid of it. It might be that you need to fulfil the tasks that are already pending as they might be consuming your energy with a hint of stress of being left undone. This card also shows that your idea might not be able to fructify soon or cannot be put into action right now, maybe due to lack of resources.

This card also shows that you might not be working on your ideas because of laziness, this also might be the cause that you have left some projects undone. You need to develop spirit of passion towards your work. Your constant putting away of work might result into people not trusting you to do their work.

Knight of Pentacles

Keywords - Action, manifesting

Personality

This knight is a sturdy personality with earthy looks and features. He has a solid view of everything he wants to do, is a chilled personality, and will go on and on in his task till he is done. He knows the nuts and bolts of fructifying plans and can figure out a way for any immature ideas/plans.

Appearance

The appearance of this card is a knight on his horse, he has a pentacle in his hands, his helmet and horses head has a green shrub depicting the growth of ideas that are going on in his head. The red reins of the horse as well as the red clothes of the knight show his grounded nature in life and while at work. There is again shown a large field sowed and ready for planting the seeds, which the knight is holding in his hands.

Meaning

The meaning of this card is that the ideas that you had in mind are now ready to be put into action. You have all that was needed to start working on this project and now it's only waiting for you to put your hands on it and start working it.

This knight is sincere in his work and steadfast, anyone can rely upon him for his abilities plus his endurance. He knows every way to bring a plan to fruition. He is not prone to get disillusioned if things don't seem to be working perfectly sometimes. He is here to win and surely does so with his work.

The card also says that you must be extremely grounded when you are at work, taking note of every detail that is happening in your environment related to your work. This also shows that you are already doing it.

The knight can be a person who looks like a really grounded person, they are normal built with shorter height and have skin colour that is of earthy tone.

This card also shows that you are in the midst of a project where everything is planned and resources are also laid for you to work upon. You just need to start taking steps further.

Reversed

When reversed this card shows delays in taking action on your carefully thought out plans. You might be facing difficulties in the middle or at the very beginning of it. This may cause a sense of anger or frustration building up, but the knight has all the keys to all the problems and so you will surely find a way out.

The reverse of this card shows that there might be scarcity of resources for making the project move further. This also might show that the deadlines that were decided previously are now likely to be extended or postponed.

This card also shows the lack of putting ones ideas into work, or you might fail to implement the right way to put things into reality. Ideas are at their best but without any promise of fulfilment.

This also shows inaction or incorrect actions. You are not able to do your work correctly due to the lack of skills to do your job.

Queen of Pentacles

Keywords - Motherly, caring

Personality

This female is an earthy coloured, stout woman who might be a housewife of might be dealing with her house well. She has this nature to pour her affection over everyone who visits her home. She is also extra caring and loving towards animals and plants around her. She always uses her money carefully and yet in such a way that all her dreams are fulfilled.

Appearance

This card appears with a woman holding a pentacle in her hands in a caring way; she is seated on a throne which has kids and fruits carved on it, which shows her affectionate nature. The fruits show her fertility and motherly nature. There is plenty of greenery around her which obviously shows earth energy at its fullest. There is a rabbit shown near her throne showing her affection and care, that a timid creature like rabbit too feels safe with her around.

Meaning

The queen is an affectionate and caring person, she might be a mother or a motherly figure; she always wants to see everyone comfortable when they are at her place. She sees to everybody's needs when they have come to her. She never tends to get angry or say no to anything. And can also feed her enemy. Considers the mantra 'a guest is God' and treats everyone with utter respect young or elder.

This card also shows the mother earth in the figure, anyone of this card personality is as humble and selfless giver as the mother earth. The Earth too takes lot of pain but only knows to nourish and nurture in return. Same is with this queen; she too takes lot of pain so that she can fulfil everybody's needs.

As this is a card of nurturing, this card also signifies that you should become independent and earn well so that you can nurture yourself. This card if appears in a spread of a person thinking of marriage then it signifies that you should get into it only if you have a steady income, otherwise become financially steady first and then make your relationship permanent.

This card also shows up when you might be too much into work, meetings and deals that you forget to take care of yourself. This card tells you that you must take care of yourself while taking all the care about your materialistic life but the key to a healthy materialistic life is first a healthy body and so take care of it first.

Reversed

When reversed this card might show carelessness, neglecting one's own needs and depression. This person might be taking too much care of others without caring for themselves. They might be giving too much of themselves that it is affecting their health. You need to take care of yourself the most, as you have the nature of nurturing many; if you would be healthy and happy then others too would be happy and their work would continue at the same pace.

Conversely this card also shows a person who doesn't take care of others, and is just involved with himself only. They are selfish and manipulative. They can help others to make their ends meet, but when their purpose is served they will vanish from the work place.

This also might show a woman who might be careless towards the family, roam about with her friends, have parties and fun but the sight of her house and housekeeping just makes her sick. She might also not be interested in bringing up her kids. Nurturing is a pain to her, instead loves when gets it from others but doesn't want to give it back.

This also might show too much of nurturing by someone in your surroundings towards you or you doing it to others; this might cause a suffocative feeling and make them feel sick in your company. You need to learn to give some space to them.

King of Pentacles

Keywords - Financial security, maturity, generous

Personality

This king is the master of this deck; he has achieved mastery over the suit of pentacles and now sits and rules. He is a medium heighted man with earthy skin tones, is in his mid-age. He holds a serene look on his face which says though being the master of this suit he is very humble and down to earth.

Appearance

This king appears with a robe that has a picture of grape vines on it, they are all ripe and are in abundance. He wears a crown with flowers and leaves woven together showing the fullness of the mother earth in all its glory. There are faces of lions on his throne which show his ruling ability as a king; there is one foot stepping outside which has armour and says he is tough from within and always ready to fight or defend when the need arises. There is shown a palace in the background, and lush greenery around him. There are also fruit plants around him showing the fruitfulness of this card, it's the final card.

Meaning

The king shows security, power, a down-to-earth person, humble and a guardian for all. He is the king, and a king is the guardian for his kingdom, who guides, protects, does justice and so on. This might be a head of the family kind of person when it is pulled out by normal people like us. The head of the family also does all of these while totally being a part of the family.

Also it's the final card of the pentacle suit which says that this person is quite a successful and rich person. He has earned a respectable position in society by virtue of his own hard work and money earned by his own abilities. He can be at a valuable position; he can be an entrepreneur, a boss, or a chairman of some leading successful business. His business is known because of him, he has earned such high self-value that people know his work because of him.

This card can show a successful achievement of any goal or task that you have undertaken. Also this means that you should be overflown by money and resources, if not yet then this card shows to continue to strive at work till you achieve a kingly position both financially and emotionally.

Also this card popping up signifies that you should be like this king and asks you to manage your tasks as well as be an authoritative figure who handles things quite well.

This king also shows that there is enough money and luxuries around you which is yours, now you can sit back and enjoy. Also the king is shown still on the throne which says that you should still keep working to maintain this position.

Reversed

When reversed this king is popular for all the wrong reasons, he might be drowning in debt, has nothing left, nor has any concern about his position or image in society. He is famous for this; people might not trust him easily as he might have fooled many in the name of money. He also has to pay off money to many and keeps running away from it giving rise to troubles to his family, who might have to constantly face people asking for money.

This person might be not at all caring or protective; it can also show a person on a high post who is heartless and cold towards people working under him. He is least bothered about anyone else then him. And his well being is the only thing that matters, when he isn't fine he would turn the whole office upside down, until a fair balance is reached.

This card also shows that you might be using money quite carelessly and there might be a danger of getting it depleted. You need to still work hard to achieve such a state where you won't need to bother much about money.

This card also shows that the king might be too much into his possessions and enjoyment of them. He might forget his duties and continue frolicking into his posh lifestyle.

This person can also be someone who is too lazy and doesn't want to work, it might be an authoritative figure who always throws all the workload on his employees and sits back and enjoys the breeze.

Beginning with your Deck

By now you must have been aware of the whole of your 78 card pack and have your journal at hand so that we can have a custom Tarot manual that's personalized to your card pack. If you are not done with it then do it first. Don't be in a hurry to learn Tarot Reading. This book is going to stay forever and so is your pack of cards. So just give yourself the leisure of diving into each card's story and learning what it stirs up into your soul as tarot is a connection to the spiritual world.

Shuffling your deck

There are various methods of shuffling your cards; I'm giving a few that I use. You can use them too or develop the way that feels right for you. You have to shuffle at the beginning of each reading. Shuffling can be simple like we do for playing cards for the rest of the day. But the first shuffle or the last shuffle should be this way, this helps the card to get mixed well and get neutralized and ready for the next reading.

All mix method

The all mix method is where you put all cards upside down and mix them a lot, letting them get reversed also. Then put these cards back into a pack and now it's ready for the reading. This method is quite a good one which can shuffle the card well with reversed and upright cards perfectly balanced according to the reading.

Cutting the Deck

You can cut the deck into half and put them into reverse position and then shuffle them to mix them well. This also is a good method but your deck should be shuffled well before placing half the cards in reverse. As your deck is arranged few suits will be reversed while the other suit completely remains upright. And we want a fuller reading which comes with randomly arranged cards.

Normal Shuffling

This is the plain shuffling method that we do while shuffling playing cards. In this method though cards should be allowed to drop, pop out, and arrange the way they have fallen. This way some cards will naturally get reversed and customized for the reading with the Querent.

How to Read the Cards, in Different ways. And how to Begin

When you are a complete beginner you feel quite excited about holding the deck, you might swiftly drive away to some magical land where you are the master of the future and when you pull out the cards and try to read them, you actually get disappointed as you didn't arrange the question well or didn't 'ask' your questions clearly or you might find the cards saying a totally different message then what your question is. I would advise to go with Tarot Reading step by step, and start with baby steps and try to grasp more and more of what your cards have depicted in the spread.

Usually a beginner understands everything what the cards are giving out only through their psyche and cannot verbalize what they mean. It is for this reason that people usually advise that you should be reading more and more stuff of Tarot rather than just one or two books. There are many books that I too have read but my mind doesn't accept the meanings of all the books. Some meanings appear quite strange to what the card is, and others give specific meanings which automatically seep into your mind. It is for this reason that Tarot Teachers around the world advice on keeping a 'tarot journal'. If you have not started writing it, start it now. It's for your own good.

Also I would like you to check various websites where you can find interesting Tarot related articles that are sometimes free or paid; you can choose any you like. Reading different people will help you hear your own psyche. Also realize what Tarot readers gel with your own thinking, once you have found out a few of them then stick to them. Learn, follow, and stay connected to them; this way you will learn more and more.

Also if you don't understand the meanings, don't give up. Keep practising daily. And keep doing for reading for yourself. Doing reading for oneself helps us understand Tarot quite quickly as we ourselves know what is in our mind, and Tarot reflects it. So we can judge very quickly how our predictions are. The meanings given are in general, you have to follow what your intuition says along with the meaning of the card. If the intuition says something very different then the card meaning then too stick to your intuition. As intuition is the master. It talks to you through the pictures.

Cards Upright & Reversed, and reading them

"Reading the Tarot is an interesting thing but it comes with a big problem. It's a complex subject which takes years to master and learn. The main question that haunts most aspirants is how to remember all the meanings if the cards." Well if this is what you have been learning from other books then stop! Tarot is not rocket science. Its as simple as knowing your own self. YES that's true. Tarot is not difficult at all. As its going to answer you through your thoughts, feelings, senses while you are trying to find answers for yourself or others.

The answer is quite simple; you don't have to remember all the meanings at all! All you have to remember is that the four elements and their properties, the major and minor arcana. If you wish you can add numerology too to the deck. Astrological associations are given, you may wish to use them now or later; it depends on you. I advice you to mug-up the four elements and their properties+which one connects to what suit.

And finally understand the meaning of each card, for *what it means to you*. I don't want you to memorize the meanings from this book neither from any other books or website. The cards are yours and when you make them individual they become uniquely yours what now no one possesses. And Praying over each card is a must for all beginners as well as advanced students. And cards can mean different things at different occasions. Just try to connect to the picture of the card and see what it has to say for that particular reading. All the meanings given may not be necessary for that question.

Praying over the card is very important. I don't say you wont get any intuitions when you don't pray. But when you form that habit, you are actually getting habituated to 'open up' to the messages that the spiritual world will be sending you during the reading.

Also the upright and reversed meanings are given, but sometimes people don't want to reverse their cards as there are equally not so good feeling cards in the deck even though they are upright. Reversed cards actually don't mean that card is negative, this really scares people; but reversed cards actually are guiding you by showing that- that particular energy is blocked and is not flowing freely. Like if lovers card is reversed you can clearly say that love energy is blocked or lovers' feeling is blocked from the life of person for whom it has appeared. So it actually will help to slowly de-tangle that block once you begin to talk out the issue with your querent.

Yet if you are compelled to use only in upright position, you can very well do so. There is nothing wrong or no drawbacks for it. The meanings of some cards in upright or reversed are shown positive while their flip side is challenging. You can choose yourself what that card in 'your' deck means good or a bad side. For instance you can follow all meanings from this side, but be open to accept to something illogical while your readings as it will take you time to get adapted to your intuition.

Court Cards and reading them

Here I come with the court cards, something that usually frets out people. Court cards are something people find difficult to predict. But according to me they are the easiest and fun when appear in the spread. We'll learn it through the best and simplest way here.

What are court cards? They are personalities, and who are these people? They are the 16 common type of people that we usually find in this world. Everybody in this world are either any one of these types. And so these personalities are the people to whom you are the client is related to, when it turns up in a reading.

First of all link a kind of personality to each suit and try to learn what feel each suit gives to you. I don't want you to follow what I feel with my cards, because this would not be fun for you; it would not bring out the real juice of intuitions Tarot brings in people.

e.g. - I like to link lean-bodied people to the suit of air as air is the least dense matter and moves quickly everywhere. So people with these qualities can be easily linked to this suit.

Then comes the suit of fire, the warm and fiery suit of Wands. I like to link people who are moderately built and athletic to this suit. As athletic built people are very much agile and active with their body movements and can do more physical work than others.

Then comes the watery suit, the quality of water is to take the shape of whatever it flows into. It keeps flowing and stays fresh and spoils when stagnates. So we can associate people who are quite chirpy and loving, bubbly to this suit. These kinds of people are found hopping here and there all the time. When they are quiet we know something is wrong, the same as the quality of water.

And finally the suit of pentacles the earthy and the most stable of all matter. These people are the ones who can sit at a place and work for hours without getting up or complaining about body-discomfort. The Earth's quality of being solid and at a pace rotating since millions of years never complaining about anything. The same is with the people of this suit.

How to frame the right questions to ask from Tarot?

Its very crucial that you ask the right questions from the Tarot. Questions should be open ended and not closed and repressed. Tarot can help us to get solutions for any situation in life and so, dull and depressing questions shouldn't be asked. Like "Is there any hope for me getting Love in future?" Well we all know that Love is meant to be available to everyone. And God himself is pure Love then why would he want anyone to stay devoid it, while its the most beautiful feeling he has created. Getting problems in relationship is a result of certain emotional or mental blocks that someone might have acquired from past experiences. Try to uplift the energy of such clients. Tell them spiritual truths about life(all good and positive stuff, don't scare them down by fears or absurd theories.) if you are not confident about giving such knowledge then try to undertake tutored courses. Good amount of quality knowledge is available for free on the internet, so try learning from there too.

So the same question about relationship can be more positive and bring better guidance from tarot in a person's life when it is open ended; for e.g- "Which is the best and quickest way to reach that Special one of my life". Now this is a question that is very powerful and will give a truly positive and empowering reading.

A correct question asked from the Tarot is like making a prediction 50% reliable just before the prediction is made.

Well why do I say that is that people who are open to get some guidance will be ready to act upon that guidance. And when a person acts there is surely going to get a result of that act. If the act is made randomly without any consultation there can be good or bad results. But with guidance from tarot you can be assured that you get guidance that will guide you to the best path that will have you to crack the soul's journey code quickly. Now when I say this it doesn't mean that you have to take Tarot guidance at every breath. Its totally not possible, and I also know of people who have been wanting me to guide this way such that they always do the ***right thing***. Well if this is the thing that people want you to do make them realize their fears about living life. Just because someone made some wrong choices in the past doesn't mean that they don't have the decision power to make right choices ever. That's wrong, totally wrong. Perhaps a person is going to learn to make better decisions in life only after few of their decisions have been terribly wrong.

Timing with Tarot

Generally people asking a tarot reading ask the *time* when a certain event can be expected to happen. This can roughly be predicted like

Wands for Days

Cups for Weeks

Swords for Months and

Pentacles for Years.

These are basically and universally accepted durations for each suit. Though I sometimes also predict swords for days, wands for weeks, cups for months and pentacles for years based on the density of each element they represent. Its totally dependent upon the intuition what it guides you to during a reading.

Spreads

Spreads are the different ways to arrange the cards in defined positions that would help you to understand the deeper meaning of the Querent's situation better. The spreads help a lot to personalize the reading according to each Querent that is laid out for. For eg- girl of 22 getting a relationship spread will bring different energy to a relationship reading whereas a woman in 30's who's divorced will bring a different energy to the same relationship spread. So the possibilities with spreads and cards is just limitless. So sit back and enjoy all the spreads, create your own, play around with different number of cards, build your own spread, build your own story after it! You can never go wrong in it. Trust your intuition its the most powerful tool that God has given you. I get many people complaining that not all people are intuitive. But that's wrong, everyone has it. Even animals have it, they all listen to it. Whereas humans are taught to forget all magical talk during infancy and made to follow schooling as the perfect guidance for life.

Spreads are many, we'll begin with basic spreads first. There are predefined spreads and then there are advanced spreads. Spreads can be varying from one card to three, five, seven, eleven or twenty one. People like sometimes to use spreads even bigger than that.

Spreads can be used defined while you are a beginner, and after practice you can design your own spread. I have created few spreads of my own here and few of them are widely used spreads. Try to use them. You can vary them according to your needs once you are easy on spreads and readings.

Reverse reading - I have made this method by myself, I don't have any idea if this method is mentioned or followed by any other tarot reader any where. Well this is quite an interesting technique. The cards that you pull out will show you direction and guidance. But sometimes they can just show you that a problematic situation was still going to last for some more time if the future cards are reversed or have a negative meaning.

And there is going to be blockage. But your querent might ask you for the solution. I believe that the cards that you pulled out themselves have the solution. I will be explaining in the three card reading spread.

Sample Readings

Here I am also giving sample readings for some of the spreads mentioned so that you get a clearer idea about how to read the cards. Well be open to what's going to come up as this will be something that you might not have expected.

Umm ok so take a deep breath and FORGET ALL THAT YOU'VE READ TILL NOW, either from this book or from anywhere else, about the tarot. As you are not going to read like other tarot readers, you are beginning to learn how to read the cards the way they are appearing to you and you are beginning to learn how your intuition is connecting to you.

For getting down to serious Tarot reading you just need to be clear in your mind to begin with. Trying to recall meanings of cards while the cards are drawn will complicate the process all the more.

One Card Reading

Here we'll discuss simple spreads beginning with one card spread. One card spread sounds quite simple? Right! You might feel that this is just a beginner's spread and choose to do it later on. But I must tell you this isn't beginners spread; it can show you a deep and vast meaning making it your entire 1 hour sitting on just this one card spread meaning.

We can either use whole of the deck to fetch this one card after shuffling or we can use only the major arcana for this reading.

Tip- Use only major arcana when a very crucial factor or decision is needed to be made, while a simple not so important question can be dealt with the full pack of 78 cards.

Also you can intend that one card will help you answer all the questions that would come up. Then with this intention shuffle and pick up one card. And then try to figure as many messages that come through that card. This might be difficult if you are a beginner but more advanced readers will be easily able to do this. Inorder to make this process 100% trustworthy the intention that you set out should be razor sharp. You can create a scared space for readings where you just do 'that' work. And then try to always read at that particular space. With time you will find that place become specific to your intuition and feel intuitional messages popping up immediately as you enter it.

Sample One-card Reading - [Identities of real people are not disclosed here.]

Question/ Issue at hand - This issue is about a girl who is currently into a serious relationship, and planning to get married soon to that person. Card pulled out is, eight of cups

Reading - The reading is simple that the situation/ relationship is a 'walk-away' kind of relationship. Though everything appears all good yet there is nothing for you in this situation. Walking away from such a situation is advisable.

Three Card Spread

The three-card spread is also a very popular spread which is commonly and widely used for simple as well as complex situations. This spread basically tells you about the past, present and future of any situation that is asked about.

A simple spread which can get quick answers to the tough questions of life, especially when you don't want to get much deeper into the situation and are concerned only about the outcome.

Sample Three-card reading

Question / Issue - This reading is for a young boy who has continuous complains about feeling low/ depressed at the flip of a hat. Cards pulled out are Three of Swords, reversed eight of pentacles and reversed knight of cups.

Reading - The reading for this guy says that in past there has severe heart-ache happened to him. He had to face it because of few people. Now I just don't predict based on the cards meanings, but also look at the picture on the card. The picture clearly says the swords have been quite sharp on his heart. And it is true he was hurt badly by his girlfriend and her friends, they humiliated him and verbally abused him.

Second card is the eight of pentacles which clearly shows that his work is getting affected because of his problem. He is currently working and has just begun his career. And the card here shows that it should be the time where he needs to build the confidence and work abilities and expertise whereas his total time is getting wasted as his mind gets drawn towards negative thoughts.

Third card again says that in future again for sometime he will be facing problems in relationships, and so he should not take another step in choosing another person as a partner. Well this is because he already is trying to get a girlfriend since the past experience but has not succeeded. And the cards say that this pattern of getting a no will still continue. So not to take any hasty decisions.

Reverse Reading - To get the answer to this issue I am doing the reverse reading. This will help me to get answer to that guys issue from the same cards which are describing these same cards.

In reverse reading you have to flip all the cards, so upright will become reversed and reversed cards will become upright. And this will be the solution to that issue.

So now the solution cards will be reversed three of swords(which brings a smile), upright eight of pentacles and upright knight of cups.

Now the reading says in-order to solve his situation of feeling dull and depressed all the time. The solution is that he has to first begin to listen to his heart. Stop hurting himself with negative thoughts(he has lots of self-esteem issues too lately, feels underrated as he doesn't have any girlfriend since years. These thoughts themselves are ruining his mind-set.) So the cards say to stop hurting you heart by the sharp hurtful thoughts of your mind(swords); Next is to begin paying serious attention to his career, begin working diligently to the tasks that lie at hand and finally he would be ready to go for a relationship that he yearns to get into.

Now when you give this solution always remember that the guidance has to be followed and made it as a habit. Its not that he would do for 2-3 days or 10 days and then is going to get a girlfriend. But after a person practices the first cards guidance for a few months(I feel swords here are pointing for months as timing), then practice the seriousness in career (this is like building a strong foundation which I feel will need years about 3-4 years after which he would be ready to go for a relationship.)

Now when you are going to give this sort of reading to someone else, you are surely going to get raised brow look. Well the cards are saying this and you need to be honest with it. And then leave it upto them whether they really accept it or not.

Five card Spread

There is also this is my favourite self-created five card spread that I'm discussing here. It helps to know people better, also the reason of their problems. The top card is first, and then comes the two other cards and finally the bottom cards. Some people like to put the cards in cross direction just to enhance their meaning and looking at the situation more closely from all directions.

- The first card is for the main hero of the issue, it's you or the Querent himself as they are asking the question.
- The second card to the right shows the active reason for the situation, querent is responsible for this
- left to the topmost card shows the passive reason/ nature's order for the situation, these two are very crucial as this will help to find out how big is the strength of the issue at hand and what forces are at play, by the Querent or through the Querent.
- And the rest of the cards show the solution the one on the right side shows what the Querent can or needs to do in this situation,
- and the left card shows what nature wants to make happen in your life and how it's going to get shaped.

Sample Reading

Issue at hand - This issue is about a lady who has been wanting to build her business and is not able to successfully put it up. This is a bit of big issue and so I chose this spread for this reading. You can choose the spread from the type of situation. As the more number of cards drawn for any reading will make it very deep and clear.

Cards pulled are- 1st Knight of Pentacles, 2nd Ace of Wands, 3rd is reversed Queen of Cups, 4th is four of swords and final 5th card is reversed knight of wands.

Reading - Here the first card is the knight of pentacles and knights are about action. They are all set to put their dreams into fulfilment by taking actions for them. A knight has already decided that he is ready to take action. So clearly we can say that the lady is this knight of pentacles. Also I must say that she has a very solid plan that will make her earn very good money. So that too reflects in the pentacles for solidity and money. As she has made her base quite solid for earning money.

2nd card says that the action that she is taking is also making her ready for her plunge into the business world. And so the ace too is not wrong here. She is responsible for the thing that is happening for bringing a block in her business. Now the ace here is actually for wands which might say that its a very good career opportunity and so most of the people would be taking it wrong as a prediction for good business; whereas the position here says why is the querent responsible for this situation. So the card clearly says that the initiative of bringing a block in the business is actually done by the querent herself. She herself steps back when she has everything ready at hand.

3rd card - the passive reason for this to happen is the reversed queen of cups, which is totally perfect at her place. This card says that the querent feels that she will be giving less time to her loved ones if she gets too businessy. And this is actually true there is everything set and if she begins she will be going busy quite a lot for first few years. Whereas she has kids where she feels she wont be giving attention to.

4th Card says the solution for this issue - The solution for this issue is that the querent can ask for Divine help to help her decide what's right for her. As this card does feel that way. Because for here being a mom is more important for her then being successful in business.

5th card is what nature wants to bring is her life. The card here is reversed knight of wands. And things are working with her in such a way that she feels giving attention to her family right now is more important rather then running after her career. As she doesn't want to repent in future about her kids' careers. So currently situations are also pointing out that she puts this idea to back seat.

Another 5 card spread

This spread is also self-designed by me, which I use quite often to find any solutions to very difficult situations/problems sometimes which seem unsolvable.

- The first card on top is the problem card that helps you to understand the problem from in and out.
- The card on right is what is acting as your weakness in the issue;
- the left card is what's boosting your weakness.
- The bottom card shows the outcome of the situation if you keep operating out of your weakness.
- The card on extreme left is the sure shot 'solution' card to this problem. This would be something that you aren't comfortable doing or it isn't your ability but doing this would help you to get out of this situation.

Sample Reading - This reading is about a guy in a well known country who is not a permanent resident and his jobs suffer just because he is not a green-card holder. He is never secure on his job and has to leave it at the drop of a hat. And he wants to get settled in the US, so he is always fearful about this situation. Cards pulled out are - 1st Page of Swords, 2nd Ace of cups, 3rd is King of Pentacles, 4th is Reversed Queen of Pentacles and 5th card is reversed Justice.

How the reading unfolds

1st card - Page of swords here show that the person in this situation is quite filled up with ideas, and does want that those ideas do fructify. But he is not about to put those ideas into action due to his residency status. He always feels arrested and lagging behind because of it, and so cannot think about putting anything into action. Which is obvious by the 'page'. The page is yearning to become a knight but unable to do that.

2nd card - The thing that boosts his weakness in this situation is that he is getting emotionally attached with the place. The lifestyle is taking a toll on him. And this is creating more of a fear for him as he doesn't want to go back to his country. This is also becoming a pain for him as his lifestyle back in his own country is not as comfortable and as good as what he's been enjoying there.

3rd card - shows his weakness in this issue. The weakness in this issue is money. He wants to earn a lot of money(as its his dream to stay well set and comfortable there) and the high aims are making him uncomfortable when he looses his job. As he feels he wont be able to cope up with that troubles and might have to give up his stay in the country.

4th card says - that if he keeps operating out of his weakness then he might have to suffer the loss of getting a permanent residency status, (which I feel is the solid base and grounding that the queen of pentacles brings)

5th Card says - what to do out of the box so that he can get what he expects, first of all justice reversed shows that there is some 'injustice' going on in the immigration department where he is reporting for his visas. And this card itself also tells me that there might be some unconventional or illegal ways by which he could apply for visas and pass quickly.

Traditional Celtic Cross Spread

The traditional Celtic Cross spread is one that is widely used all over the world by most of Tarot Readers. You too will love it due to the depth it gives on any situation.

* The first card the bottommost card is the situation card,
* the 2nd is for you in this situation,
* the 3rd is for what is crossing this situation,
* the 4th card is foundation of this situation and how deep it is,
* the 5th card is the past, 6th card is the present and the
* 7th card is the future;
* the 8th stands for yourself,
* the 9th for your environment,
* the 10th is for hopes and fears and
* the 11th is for outcome.

This is a very powerful tool to find answers, to the toughest questions/ problems.

Sample Reading with Celtic Cross - This reading is done for general purposes for someone who didn't ask me any questions. The lady just wanted to help me understand her life better and give some advice based on that. So I chose a celtic cross spread.

1st card - The first card shows her and how she is feeling about herself currently. The king in reversed position showed me that she is the king but felt very passive about her life. She also felt that though she is the master of her life she still was not able to rule it. And it for sure was this way, she is a housewife and felt that she wasn't doing or being the actual kingly self that she is.

2nd card is the herself in this situation reversed eight of pentacles, this card also almost shows what she feels. And why she feels that way. She has lot of abilities and yet feels passive as she was not working. She was helping her hubby in his business but that wasn't giving her any recognition as compared to what input she was giving in the work.

3rd Card here is for what is crossing the situation reversed knight of cups, the card shows that there is some emotional relationship or bondage that is stopping her from doing what she wants. This young person is probably her young son at the university who is not staying close to her.

This along with the fees that the university might be needing is making her feel unfulfilled about her situation.

4th Card here is for the foundation of this situation, this is the nine of cups card. I feel that this man is sitting and feels sitting is a form of joy. The sitting I feel corresponds to the passivity of her in this situation also her being a housewife. The man I feel who think is her hubby. Her hubby feels a woman sitting at home is the queen of the house etc. And its an honour for a woman to be titled as a Housewife. This is the base of this situation. So whatever passivity that this woman is experiencing its root cause is her being a housewife.

5th Card is for the past with a reversed Devil, this card says that she has been trying to untangle herself from the ties of the beliefs of her hubby. And this is making her feel more better for herself.

6th card showing her present situation is the knight of pentacles, which screams a super duper confident lady that was in front of me. She is all well set to set her own brand for something, I felt its home based business and is already in succession for it.

7th Card for future shows ten of wands shows the very obvious net possibility of her career that she will be working hard for the net few months or about few years to give her business a strong base.

8th Card is for herself which shows by the reversed wheel of fortune, this card I feel is actually showing a blockage in the changing of fortune for her. This blockage might be because she might be needing to work hard first for the project at hand and then she can expect this card to appear upright.

9th Card is for her environment is the reversed Tower. Tower here is reversed showing some good signs. I don't feel that she will have to jump out of her house in-order to do what she wants. The people around her would be supportive and helpful. Especially her husband, he would be supportive for her. Though what she is doing is completely against her beliefs.

10th Card is for the hopes and fears - this is the ace of wands card, a pretty healthy card to receive in this position. Good business and she can hope this business to flourish.

11th card is for outcome, and its the four of swords - now this card I feel here is telling me that she is the man who is lying down and praying. I feel this points towards that she should have trust and have faith in the divine that he would bring her success for all the endeavours that he has made her to dream about.

Similarly you can do the reading for these spreads too. I am not explaining all of them. Instead I have left some space for you to complete these exercises. I feel it would be fun to do it. Isnt it?

Health Spread

The Health Spread is to be taken in general, never give health reading to people suffering from serious illnesses as it may be risky because these people usually have a severely damaged system which requires intense care, and they sometimes just want to depend on predictions for living(Ive come across many of these, who just depend on my prediction. So I stopped giving out readings for health). Advise them to contact a Medical Practitioner. Never ever advice/ prescribe unless you too are a qualified Medical Doctor. Also ask them to take proper medication, rest as per experts advice to get healed.

The instructions on the right show how you can go through the spread with someone wanting general health advice.

Try to be specific as well as soothing and comforting in your advice. Remember people always know what's good and what's not, it's just that they are now ready to know and accept it consciously.

Reading

Career Reading

Career Reading for students of schools and colleges, try to be very specific while giving advice; know their field of interests so that you can get more specific with your advice.

Also try to figure out whether it's the field they like or someone related to them, likes that field. This kind of thinking or coaxing will just lead to confusion and blocking of mind.

Remember you are not a career consultant, but a Tarot Reader. You may not have ideas about all careers out there. So it's okay if you need to ask your client's about their interests.

Yes you can do the homework optionally of collecting information and doing some research on regular basis about different careers and their eligibilities and requirements. In order to give fuller readings and advises to your clients.

Reading

Wealth Reading

The Wealth Spread gives you an idea about people and their money.

This spread will be usually demanded by all. But only few will really come to you with a real goal to become millionaires.

This can be confusing as all would demand and say they want a lot of money. This is because they actually have lot of problems and wish for abundance so that they can wash away their financial problems in just one swish.

Try to make your client understand what their actual wish is. And ask them to handle current money problems tactfully.

Also do clear out blockages about money there can be fears, hatred etc feelings for money based on what you have been hearing about it most of the time from people around you.

Reading

Relationship Reading

The Relationship reading is also a common reading all will want to get, this is tricky sometimes in one- sided relationships as well as fun in some good pairing. This relationship reading is for anyone. It can be done for partners, parent-child relationship, brother-sister relationship, two friends etc.

Reading

The Fool's Journey or Soul's Journey Spread

This spread is self-created too. This is different and can be done with only Major Arcana or with full pack of minor arcana. Another variation is you can do this only with Minor Arcana too, to find out where you are in the more practical world.

The fool's journey as you remember I explained in beginning of this book. The Fool's journey applies to the learning of a person during this life and also the Soul's journey across lifetimes. So to make the reading more clear you can use the variations of Major arcana, all cards or just Minor Arcana cards.

This spread will be done shuffling all the cards together. And then put a centre card choosing a card faced down from the pack. This will be the fool's place. Which card comes up, you can judge according to its meaning what's the beginning point of that journey. It can be any major or minor card just be open to receive any of them.

And around this card place other 21 card. These 1-21 cards will be in exact same order as there are the 21 cards of major Arcana. I mean they will be ***acting out*** as those cards according to what is going on in the querent's life at that time.

Sample Reading - I will not be giving the entire reading but just first few cards, just to give an idea about how this reading should be done. Here I am doing a sample reading with Major Arcana Cards only. This is done for a lady who is very much having knowledge about spirituality and she wanted to know where is she on the fool's journey path. This will help us to know how much has her awareness developed.

The fool's place is occupied by the Hanged man, which means at the position where she should be having a faith inside her to take the leap into the unknown. To take that step from one world to the other world she is at a place where she is in a limbo period. She feels she cannot do anything to move or budge from that situation. A feeling of being stuck and not being able to take the leap just because she is tied upside down to the tree trunk.

The magician's place is occupied by the Tower, which is oopss... The place which shows her that the magical abilities that she possesses and can work with them is actually struck by a thunderbolt and she is pushed out of that area. Her creativity is being pushed out and made to think that its not needed or its useless. Its actually because you feels it is that way.

The high priestess' place is taken by wheel of fortune which actually feels good. As the leap of faith is not been taken by the fool because he might feel that the magicians place isn't worthy of anything. But the high priestess says that her spiritual abilities or intuition are going to have a fortunate twist in upcoming time. This would be life changing for her.

I guess now you must have understood how this reading is to be done, so I am not explaining all the 22 cards here. As it might take too much of space. You can go along and practice the rest of the reading. Here's the rest of the cards.

3rd card - Devil, 4th -Hermit, 5th - Judgement, 6th - Fool, 7th - The Star, 8th - Chariot, 9th Card - Temperence, 10th Card - Hierophant, 11th Card - Endings/beginnings, 12th - Strength, 13th - The Empress, 14th Card - Justice, 15th Card - World, 16th - Lovers, 17th - Moon, 18th - Sun, 19th - High Priestess, 20th - Magician, 21st - Emperor.

Tarot Mini Guide – Major Arcana

The Fool

Element- Air

Keywords- Live freely, take risks, beginnings, winding up, a fresh start, travelling, taking a new adventure, trusting the universe, be carefree towards troubles....

The Magician

Planetary association- Mercury

Keywords- Creating magic with your abilities, working out fully one's potential, a career of your choice, using your talents to work magic.

The High Priestess

Planetary association – Ruled by Moon

Keywords- Intuition, inner-guidance, trust yourself, secrets to be revealed or kept

The Empress

Ruled by- Venus

Keywords- Abundance of resources, femininity, motherhood

The Emperor

Ruled by- Aries

Keywords- Dominance, power, ruler, leadership, fatherhood, tyranny

The Hierophant

Ruled by - Taurus

Keywords - Studying, teaching, getting a guru, learning

The Lovers

Ruled by - Gemini

Keywords-Love, romance, dreams come true, follow your heart, marriage, romance, life partner, dream job

The Chariot

Ruled by - Cancer

Keywords - Taking charge, balancing negative and positive polarities, taking control of one's life

Strength

Ruled by- Leo

Keywords- Control, bravery, stamina, daring, will power

The Hermit

Ruled by- Virgo

Keywords- Inner reflection, loneliness, step after introspecting carefully, continue moving ahead...

Wheel of Fortune –

Ruled by- Jupiter (The biggest of all planets, shows the power of this card)

Keywords- Turn of time wheel, change in fortune, drastic changes

Justice

Ruled by- Libra

Keywords- Justice, nature's justice, law, principles

The Hanged Man

Ruled by- Neptune

Keywords- Limbo period, wait and watch, trapped feeling, look things differently

Death

Ruled by- Scorpio

Keywords- Death, transformation, extreme change, unacceptable changes, cleansing of the old.

Temperance

Ruled by- Sagittarius

Keywords- Stay balanced at difficult times, handle delicate matters carefully, and control your temperament.

Devil

Ruled by- Capricorn

Keywords- Bonding, imprisonment, attachment, lust, greed

Tower

Ruled by- Mars

Keywords- Breakdown, unexpected chaos, break beliefs

The Star

Ruled by- Aquarius

Keywords- Healing, hope, humility, take things as they come to you, letting go, dream fulfilment

The Moon

Ruled by- Pisces

Keywords- Fear, hidden dangers, surprises, uncertainty of what lies ahead, subconscious mind, cool moon energy.

The Sun

Ruled by- The Sun

Keywords- Positivity, activity, rejoicing, life

Judgment

Ruled by- Pluto

Keywords- Release of unwanted, past life connections, rise high, karma paying time (has come or is over)

World

Ruled by- Saturn

Keywords- Success, end of a phase happily, triumph, balance of all elements in your life, success in projects or endeavours

Minor Arcana
Suit of Swords

Suit of swords represents the air element, personalities of this suit will be fugitive, impatient, and always mobile; this suit carries the energy of unsteadiness of mind leading to problems....

Ace of Swords

Keywords – New idea, thought

Two of Swords

Keywords – Not able to judge, confusion, blindfolded

Three of Swords

Keywords – Mind against heart, walk your heart's way

Four of Swords

Keywords- Restlessness, fear, insecurity

Five of Swords

Keywords- Fight, always winning attitude, put down people, never accept your defeat.

Six of Swords

Keywords- Travelling, safe journey, bright future across the seas.

Seven of Swords

Keywords- Stealing of ideas, objects, treachery

Eight of Swords

Keywords- Blinded vision, lack of clarity, confusion, tied-up feeling, restricted movements.

Nine of Swords

Keywords- Crying, great sorrow, guilt, misery, difficult or dark times, dark night of the soul.

Ten of Swords

Keywords- Back stabbing, betrayal, health crisis, resting period

Page of Swords

Keywords- Restless, hyperactive, can't be steady at once place for long time

Personality- This can be a young child male/female with slim body (as they are very active), they will show these qualities very often. Also adults and elderly people can show these qualities.

Knight of Swords

Keywords- Pace, hasty, high temper, quick actions, hates slowing

Personality- This can be an adult person male/female lean bodied, with the qualities listed. It can also be a very young person trying to behave as such or a very elderly person who shows these qualities.

Queen of Swords

Keywords- Dominance, power, sharp mind, decisive, strong willed, independent

Personality- This lady can be a middle-aged female with the qualities given above, full body, also it can be a very young person male/female who might be displaying such qualities and maturity.

King of Swords

Keywords- Agile, sharp minded, sharp tongued, in conquerable mental abilities, unconquerable verbally/ by wit/ or intelligence wise, mastermind

Personality- This is a male/female tall and lean bodied, appears quite restless from their structure, this can also show young adults with these qualities but with the perfection of the air suit.

Suit of Wands

Wands are the fiery suit, the fiery passion and drive to achieve goals, to do something in life to make world know you, career and alike..... Personalities of this suit are passionate, hard-working, ambitious, steadfast.

Ace of Wands

Keywords- Beginning a project, initiating work, new step further

Two of Wands

Keywords- Give out, globalize, open doors, sharing your talents/abilities with the world

Three of Wands

Keywords- Waiting, wait for the world to respond, anticipation

Four of Wands

Keywords- Family, marriage, celebration, rejoicing, reunion

Five of Wands

Keywords- Fight, clash in views, controversy, conflict

Six of Wands

Keywords- Victory, applause, fame, praise

Seven of Wands

Keywords- Safeguarding, building a wall, fear, stopping, stopping something from flowing

Eight of Wands

Keywords- Communication, media, speed, pace

Nine of Wands

Keywords- Insecurity, fears, panic, safeguard, shielding

Ten of Swords

Keywords- Working hard, workload, career at fullest, persistence

Page of Wands

Keywords- Enthusiasm, passion about to flow, creative thoughts

Personality- This person would be of medium to tall height, with an athletic build, not too heavy and neither too slim. Skin can be peachy colour to all medium tones. They are centred people looking quite calm but have an ocean of creativity to learn something new, to discover something new runs within.

Knight of Wands

Keywords- Pace in career, speedy success, passion, ambition, dream come true

Personality

This person is a fiery natured person who wants his dreams to come true at all costs, he is ready to devote time, energy and persists till he gets what he wants. He can work 24 × 7 for fulfilling his dream, he's an athletic built charismatic person that steals attention wherever he passes from. A warm-hearted, affectionate person; medium-tall and well built, earthy skin tones.

Queen of Wands

Keywords- Artistic, friendly, tough, articulate

Personality

This female has a tough athletic body; she is a warm & affectionate person with tough looks. She believes in the here and now. She is friendly, believes in building faith in people. There's no task that's tough for her. She is career minded at the same time is a very good human being.

King of Wands

Keywords- Patient listener, hard to escape, work is worship.

Personality

A moderately tall, athletic built person, this person is of peachy-wheatish coloured skin tone. They are tough looking with a soft heart. They have love for their work and goals inbuilt in them. They like to reward people for doing their work; they are entrepreneurs, bosses, CEO's of huge organizations.

Suit of Cups

Cups are the watery suit, and as water flows so do the emotions flow either the ones that feel good or not feeling good. The cups carry the energy of healing and love with it. Personalities linked with this suit are very loving, sensitive, and affectionate people.

Ace of Cups

Keywords- Love energy enters, new relationship, gift of love

Two of Cups

Keywords- Partners, soul mates, friendship, new partnership.

Three of Cups

Keywords- Celebration, rejoicing, party, marriage, get-together

Four of Cups

Keywords- Unaccepting, self-punishment, resentment, stubbornness

Five of Cups

Keywords- Crying, whining, loss, let-go

Six of Cups

Keywords- Sharing, giving love or whatever you have ample of, meeting people

Seven of Cups

Keywords- Choices, options, dreaming, wishes

Eight of Cups

Keywords- Detachment, walking away, spiritual search

Nine of Cups

Keywords- Pride, satisfaction, sit back, contentment, achievement

Ten of Cups

Keywords- Joy, completeness, family happiness

Page of Cups

Keywords- New thought for love, new idea about love life

Personality

This might be a young person or a child who is very sensitive and loving and caring at nature. Caring and affectionate they win hearts with their talks. Fair to wheatish fair complexioned. They can also be dark complexioned but having the same qualities about love as above.

Knight of Cups

Keywords- Passion, romantic, affectionate, caring

Personality

The knight is a person with a drive of passion to live to his dreams. He wishes something and then works towards fulfilling it; he is much passionate about it.

Queen of Cups

Keywords- Nurturer, loving, compassionate

Personality

This queen is quite a loving person and caring. They would be very good human's probably the best kind of humans. They deal people with utter respect, hardly get hurt by anyone as people would never like to hurt anyone like them. They are usually healers, doctors and all everyone dealing with emotions and feelings.

King of Cups

Keywords- Balanced person, focused, humble, and compassionate

Personality

This is a quite humble looking person, his face drips with compassion and care, he is always ready to give a helping hand. A mature aged man with a heavy body, love for sweets, skin may be fair to wheatish.

Suit of Pentacles

Pentacles is the earthy suit with a lot of down-to-earthiness, solid base, materialism, money, health flowing through it, it may also mean lack of these in some cases. Personalities of this suit are like the qualities of earth, warm, calm, moving slowly but steadily.

Ace of Pentacles

Keywords- Opportunity to earn money, gaining money & resources

Two of Pentacles

Keywords- Juggling, manifestation on a hold, careful handling of money/resources

Three of Pentacles

Keywords- Orders, designing, focus on work

Four of Pentacles

Keyword- Save money/resources, possessiveness, holding on, greed, miser

Five of Pentacles

Keywords- Poverty, lack, crisis, helpless

Six of Pentacles

Keywords- Donation, helping, giving

Seven of Pentacles

Keywords- Waiting, investment

Eight of Pentacles

Keywords- Self-employment; using one's ability, skills, talents

Nine of Pentacles

Keywords- Abundance, plenty, pleasures

Ten of Pentacles

Keywords- Richness, luxury, windfall, financial stability

Page of Pentacles

Keywords- New job opportunity, money growing ideas

Personality

This page has a personality of a very steady and quiet person; they are builders they will always try to build something or the other. This kid might show up interest in playing games that involves building blocks and alike. The child might have characteristics of being quiet and maybe too easy going and cool headed. But they are very good at persistence; they can keep working on something until it is finished.

Knight of Pentacles

Keywords- Action, manifesting

Personality

This knight is a sturdy personality with earthy looks, and features. He has a solid view of everything he wants to do. He is a chilled personality and will go on and on in his task till done. He knows the nuts and bolts of fructifying plans and can figure out way for any immature ideas/plans.

Queen of Pentacles

Keywords- Motherly, caring

Personality

This female is an earthy-coloured, stout woman who might be a housewife of might be dealing with her house well. She has this nature to pour her affection over everyone who visits her home. She is also extra caring and loving towards the animals and plants around her. She always uses her money carefully and yet in such a way that all are fulfilled.

King of Pentacles

Keywords- Financial security, maturity, generous

Personality

This king is the master of this deck; he has achieved mastery over the suit of pentacles and now sits and rules. He is a medium-heighted man with earthy skin tones, is in his mid-age. He holds a serene look on his face which says though being the master of this suit he is very humble and down to earth.

Tarot Resources

The best Tarot website is www.aeclectic.net which has almost all Tarot Decks ever published listed on it. You can browse alphabetically, theme wise and also publication wise. It also has listed the world's best Tarot Books which is also convenience if you want to read more tarot books. I have my Tarot Card meanings given at http://www.tarot-angel-reading.com/learntarot which you can check out.

Best Tarot Author's

1. Rachel Pollack
2. Mary K. Greer
3. Barbara Moore
4. Joan Bunning (with her learning tarot website www.learntarot.com)
   And many more.... You'll get more info on www.aeclectic.net

Recommended Advanced Decks

* Shadowscapes Tarot by Stephanie Pui Mun Law
* Lo Scarabeo Tarot by Lo Scarabeo
* Legacy of the Divine Tarot by Ciro Marchetti
* Gilded Tarot by Ciro Marchetti
* Angel Tarot, Guardian Angel Tarot by Doreen Virtue

Also check top-ten Tarot Decks at www.aeclectic.net if you dont like these decks much. There are more then 1500 decks listed there along with sample pics.

My Websites & Services

You can check my services and courses on my websites, and also the blog where regular informative articles are posted; you might like to read. Also subscribe to newsletter to get regular tips, tricks and informational articles about Tarot, Angels and above all about Life itself. I would love to know how you liked this book so please connect to me and let me know.

www.nirvana-now.in

www.tarot-angel-reading.com

Connect with me on Facebook & Youtube to get regular updates for Tarot and other courses -

www.facebook.com/tarotangelreading

www.facebook.com/nirvananow.in